PRAISE FOR

Sex, God, and the Brain

"This book is so much fun. *Sex, God, and the Brain* examines ground-breaking research to turn common perceptions about sexuality and spirituality on its head. A must-read for anyone looking to better understand the profound relationship between sex and religion. Well-researched and deeply insightful." —**Daniel Amen, *New York Times* bestselling author of *Change Your Brain, Change Your Life***

"Rigorous science wildly upends conventional thought. Here Dr. Andrew Newberg creates a highly scholarly and evocative new scientific paradigm, that compels reexamination of our foundational human nature. He asks what might be the paths to awakening human perception of the unitive reality? How do different people arrive to this awareness, and is it really the same awareness? Do these paths intertwine, do they work, and if so, how?

"Newberg's innovation is matched by his scientific precision to evoke a compelling inquiry, as he allows research to kick-open a door hitherto sealed by societal norms. Hold on tight! You are in the seat of a fearless, brilliant investigator." —**Lisa Miller, PhD, Columbia University professor and bestselling author, *The Awakened Brain: The New Science of Spirituality and Our Quest for an Inspired Life***

"Groundbreaking work on understanding the fundamental link between sexuality and spirituality, and essential reading for understanding how and why sexuality is so important for our spiritual well-being. Newberg makes complex research readable and fun for everyone and helps show how our brain is the connection between the spiritual and biological self. Respecting both science and the spiritual, this book is an instant classic." —**Sara Gottfried, M.D., *New York Times* bestselling author of *The Hormone Cure***

"Newberg's book deftly interweaves neurobiology, theology, sociology, psychology, philosophy, sexuality, and history to explore the very essence of the human experience. Dichotomously in-depth but digestible, this book is a must-read for anyone wanting to understand how religion and sexuality interplay with the evolution of human society." —**Billicent "Billy" San Juan, PsyD, Author and Educator**

Sex, God, and the Brain

Also by Andrew Newberg

Sex, God, and the Brain

HOW SEXUAL PLEASURE GAVE BIRTH TO RELIGION AND A WHOLE LOT MORE

ANDREW NEWBERG, M.D.

TURNER

PUBLISHING COMPANY

Turner Publishing Company

Nashville, Tennessee

www.turnerpublishing.com

Cover design: Faceout Studios

Book Design: William Ruoto

Library of Congress Cataloging-in-Publication Data
Names: Newberg, Andrew B., 1966- author.
Title: Sex, God, and the brain : how sexual pleasure gave birth to religion
   and a whole lot more / Andrew Newberg, M.D.
Description: Nashville, Tennessee : Turner Publishing, [2024] | Includes
   bibliographical references and index.
Identifiers: LCCN 2023040643 (print) | LCCN 2023040644 (ebook) | ISBN
   9781684428618 (hardcover) | ISBN 9781684428625 (paperback) | ISBN
   9781684428632 (epub)
Subjects: LCSH: Sex—Religious aspects.
Classification: LCC BL65.S4 N495 2024 (print) | LCC BL65.S4 (ebook) | DDC
   202/.12—dc23/eng/20240126
LC record available at https://lccn.loc.gov/2023040643
LC ebook record available at https://lccn.loc.gov/2023040644

Printed in the United States of America

1 2 3 4 5 6 7 8 9 10

To my parents, wife, and daughter,

all of whom are part of the web of

life, both biological and spiritual,

with me.

CONTENTS

SEX AND GOD

[If humans] were deprived of the [sexual instinct] ... all ambition, endeavor, and affection, all poetry, art, and religion—in short, all the emotions and achievements inspired by what we term *love* would cease, and the world would become cold and passionless; destitute of sentiment or aspiration, devoid of any incentive to progress or energy; while the intricate and reciprocal machinery of human society, robbed of its motive force, would come to a stop and crumble away in hopeless disorganization. It is universally admitted that love is the animating spirit of the world; and what is love but a manifestation of the sexual instinct?

—Clifford Howard in *Sex Worship*

WHY SEX AND GOD?

In the pages that follow, you are going to learn about an astonishing conclusion—that religions derive from sex. If you stop for a moment to consider it, this actually makes a great deal of sense since the elements of religion—rituals, beliefs, experiences, and worship—all share the same basic brain functions that are involved with sex and mating. In the pages that follow, you will come to learn about the latest research that links sexuality and spirituality, and find out how the evolutionary power of sex led humanity down a profound philosophical and theological path.

I want to state clearly up front that identifying the association between sex and religion is not meant in any way to denigrate religion but instead to show its powerful link to the most basic of all drives at the core of our being. This conclusion helps us understand how and why religion is so powerful whether you believe in God or not. If you believe, it makes sense that religion would be connected at a primal level to the most fundamental of all activities for a species. And if you do not believe, it has to be admitted that religion has been around since the beginning of humanity, and thus, should be embedded deep within the evolutionary forces that shaped the human brain and being.

But let's start with a simple question: Have you ever noticed the unusual obsession that religions seem to have with sex? In large part, monotheistic religions are quite opinionated on the topic of sex. For these traditions, sex is often something that is only for having babies and is not meant to be fun. Many Christian groups from the Catholics to the Puritans have related sex to an extremely specific and pragmatic purpose—being fruitful and multiplying. In Catholicism, sex outside of marriage is a sin that will send you straight to Hell. And if one dedicates their life to become a priest or nun, they vow never to have sex again. The other monotheistic traditions are also pretty clearly against sex or sexuality if it is only for personal pleasure. In Islam, particularly those who follow Sharia law, women are prohibited from tempting men sexually to such a strong degree that they must be covered from head to toe. Orthodox Jews similarly have strong beliefs about sexuality, especially when it comes to a woman's menstrual period. Women must go to a Mikvah bath to cleanse themselves after their menstrual period, and cannot engage in sex until they are sufficiently purified. Imagine that . . . a natural biological function such as menstruation requires a purification ritual!

Why are these religious traditions so afraid of sex, and why have they gone to such great lengths to deal with sex in very specific ways?

Before answering that question, we have to acknowledge that not all traditions are opposed to sex and sexuality. Some of the earliest religions had their foundations in sexuality and fertility. Historical evidence of this includes one of the oldest known pieces of art believed to represent a fertility goddess with prominent buttocks and breasts, and there are many phallic symbols that abound throughout ancient religions.[1] From the tall obelisks of ancient temples, to the worship of mountains and reverence of animals with particularly strong sexual abilities, human spirituality has long

---

1   Scott GR. *Phallic Worship: A History of Sex and Sexual Rites.* Luxor Press; 1966.

centered on sexual symbols and the sexual act. Hundreds of thousands of years ago, human beings obviously understood the importance and power of sex. Ancient creation myths describe how supernatural beings had sex in order to give birth to the universe. In fact, all gods, including the monotheistic God, are primarily defined by their creative prowess. As Clifford Howard put it in his 1909 book, *Sex Worship*, "Brahma, Jehovah, God, Allah and hundreds of others, are simply different names for the same deity, as viewed from different standpoints; and this deity, this universal object of adoration, is the supreme creative power."[2]

The ancient Greeks were no exception, and their Mount Olympus appears to have been a pretty provocative place. Greek myths frequently included sex between gods and also between gods and human beings. The term *mount* not only refers to mountains but also derives from the Greek, *mons*, which refers to the fleshy protuberance just above the female pubic bone called the *mons pubis*. Finally, the verb *mount* refers to the initiation of sexual intercourse in which the male mounts the female. There will be much more about these topics discussed later.

Many traditions throughout the world, both ancient and present, have focused on phallic worship—recognizing the importance of the penis with regard to mating and reproduction. Phallic worship is seen almost everywhere from the straight and strong columns of Greek and Roman temples to the overt sexual imagery of ancient Hindu art. Phallic imagery is so prevalent that many people in the monotheistic traditions don't always recognize the phallic oriented symbols and worship practices that are displayed before them daily.

In Judaism, one of the primary ways in which the covenant with God is confirmed is through the act of male circumcision. In Genesis 17:9-11 (NIV), we learn about the manner in which God makes a covenant with Abraham: "As for you, you must keep my covenant, you and your descendants after you for the generations to come. This is my covenant with you and your descendants after you, the covenant you are to keep: Every male among you shall be circumcised. You are to undergo circumcision, and it

---

2   Howard C. *Sex Worship: An Exposition of the Phallic Origin of Religion*. Chicago Medical Book Co.; 1909: 32-33.

will be the sign of the covenant between me and you."[3] God goes further to state that any male who is not circumcised will be cut off from his people (no pun intended) since it breaks the covenant. The reason for invoking the importance of circumcision is itself a realization of the importance of the penis, which a person would touch when making a commitment or oath. Have you ever noticed a remarkable similarity between the words *testicle* and *testify*? It may be no coincidence. It is believed that the action of touching one's genitals when making some type of oath or covenant might directly symbolize swearing on your progeny.[4]

In Christianity, the cross has often been linked to a phallic symbol for its straightness and the off-center position of the horizontal component. However, the cross is not unique to Christianity. Crosses have been used as religious symbols dating back over 50,000 years to the upper paleolithic period. They have also represented fundamental cosmological and astronomical concepts. The other key relationship between Christianity and sexuality is the notion of the Father and the Son, and the virgin birth. There is a clear lineage represented therein, with unique and powerful creative overtones. In Christianity, as with all monotheistic traditions, God is regarded as the "parent" of the universe.

In Islam, the minarets of most mosques are obvious phallic symbols. They are large tubular structures with openings at the top. While they function to show ascendancy and power, as well as the practical aspect as a watch tower, it has been suggested that minarets are the architectural representation of Islamic pride in their founder Ishmael's self-circumcision. The male aspects of the minarets are also counterbalanced with the domes of the mosques which represent the feminine genitalia.

Eastern traditions have also engaged sexuality in substantial ways. In Hinduism, particularly the tantric sects, sexuality was to be part of the human spiritual experience and a path toward spiritual enlightenment. In addition, sexuality leads to the soul's rebirth and the ongoing cycle of

---

3   Bible Hub. Bible. New International Version. Biblica, Inc.°; 2011. Accessed March 18, 2023. https://biblehub.com/niv/genesis/17.htm.

4   Pilch JJ. *A Cultural Handbook to the Bible*. William B. Eerdmans Publishing Company; 2012.

Atman. In Buddhism, sex is often considered an important part of spirituality. For example, Tantric Buddhism is known for the sexual practices of its adherents, who strive to transform erotic passion into spiritual ecstasy and bliss.[5]

It would certainly stand to reason that sex, an act fundamental to human existence, would have significant attention paid to it by religions over the course of history. But is it just that sex is important to human beings, and that is why it plays a prominent role in religion? Or is there possibly something more?

Is it possible that the underlying neuronal connections for religion and spirituality are the same ones used for sex?

THE BRAIN, SEXUALITY, AND SPIRITUALITY

In this book, we will explore the idea that spirituality and sexuality share the same neurobiological basis in the brain. To do so, we will consider that this intimate connection is a major contributor to the challenge that sex poses for religions. Some religions see sex as literally competing for the same feelings as spiritual ecstasy. Maybe this is amusingly evidenced by so many people shouting, "Oh God!" during sex. Thus, sex should be avoided at all costs other than for the absolutely necessary reason of procreation and carrying on the community, and ultimately, the species. There is actually an entire theology of sexuality with all kinds of discussions and rules about sex—when to have it, how to have it, what to do after you have it, and implications for morality.[6] Saints, popes, and philosophers throughout history have considered sexuality in the context of religion and tried to argue, based on sacred texts and philosophy, how sex should be regarded. Of course, as mentioned previously, some religious and spiritual groups have realized the potential of sexuality in helping people turn on these spiritual circuits. In this way, sexuality has the potential to enable people to be more

---

5   Shaw M. *Passionate Enlightenment: Women in Tantric Buddhism*. Princeton University Press; 2022.

6   Rogers EF Jr, ed. *Theology and Sexuality*. Blackwell Publishers Ltd; 2002.

spiritual and possibly achieve heightened spiritual experiences or even enlightenment.

There is another important point that arises from the discussion about how sexuality and religion overlap in the brain. It is not only that sexuality and religion have similar neurobiological origins, but that this fact may help explain the evolutionary basis of religion. In fact, sexuality might be the reason that we have religion in the first place, at least evolutionarily speaking. There is also a philosophical basis for this relationship, as it might have something to do with Plato's notion of reconnecting with the other part of our self. As Plato described in *The Symposium*, "According to Greek mythology, humans were originally created with four arms, four legs and a head with two faces. Fearing their power, Zeus split them into two separate parts, condemning them to spend their lives in search of their other halves."

Perhaps sexuality is the way in which we biologically find the other half of our self, and religion is the way in which we spiritually find the other half of our self—our connection with God or some ultimate reality.

Thus, sexuality and mating, the basis of all evolutionary processes, may lead humanity down a spiritual or religious path.

Of course, as I alluded to earlier, one can always argue from the religious perspective that if God exists, it makes sense that the brain would have a mechanism by which we can understand God, interact with God, and pray to God. After all, it would be fundamentally silly for God to exist and to create human beings without giving them any way of understanding or knowing God. But if this were true, it does not mean that there has to be a special apparatus in the brain that enables us to be religious. In fact, all of the evidence to date shows that the brain has many functions that have dual purposes. For example, we don't have a language part of the brain for everyday language and a separate language part of the brain for reading sacred texts like the Bible or Quran. And if we feel love for God, and for someone else, we don't have two different love areas in the brain. We use the same brain areas for both religious and nonreligious activities. On the other hand, there does seem to be something unique about religion and spirituality. We identify religious beliefs and experiences as *different* from other beliefs and experiences.

So, what is it that specifically makes religion feel so religious?

This book aims to answer that question. But this book also goes one step further. While the religious view of how the brain became religious makes sense if you are a believer, if you believe that religion came about as part of the evolutionary process, you might have to come up with another, evolutionarily-based explanation. Exploring the relationship between sexuality and spirituality may offer an answer to how religion got into the brain regardless of your personal beliefs. In this book, we will consider both spiritual and evolutionary answers.

TAKING IT FROM HERE

In the following pages, I will give a detailed account of groundbreaking research associated with a unique spiritual practice called Orgasmic Meditation (OM), a ritualized clitoral stroking technique that has been taught to over 40,000 people around the world. The research involved high-tech functional brain scans of forty Orgasmic Meditation practitioners. When reviewed, the scans clearly demonstrated an overlap in brain structures that have to do with sexual and spiritual experience.

I also want to be clear that while I find it fascinating to study practices such as OM, in addition to those from many other groups and traditions, I do not personally endorse any of them. There are many paths to spiritual experiences and each person must find the one that is right for them. I do hope that this research helps people to understand how these practices work and provides the impetus for finding an approach that supports their own spiritual journey, wherever it may take them.

That all being said, OM is a twenty-first-century technique for self-realization that came out of the Bay Area in the 1960s. OM has an interesting and complex theoretical foundation, drawing from Reichian therapy, Daoism, and classical Tantra, which is reflected within stories that will be related throughout this book from OM practitioners discussing the spiritual experiences they've had during the practice. In addition, we will review how the subjective experiences connect with what is going on in the brain during OM, and we will see how the OM data connects with my original research into the neuroscience of spiritual states.

From the high-tech MRI and PET brain scans of OM practitioners and practitioners of other spiritual practices, and what they tell us about the human brain, you may find it surprising, but it is quite important to explore how these findings relate to the development of animal mating rituals. In doing so, we will find similar neurobiological signatures in OM practitioners today to those that likely created the warm, fuzzy feelings in animals dating back eons ago. In chapter 2, we will examine those behaviors in light of brain evolution, looking at the ways animal mating rituals carry over into human ritualistic behavior. This chapter will also explore how mating rituals in animals created the neurological framework for the development of myth, prophesy, divination, experiences of transcendent states, and models of reality.

Chapter 3 will consider the relatively recent development, at least evolutionarily speaking, of organized religions, which formalized prehistoric ritual and myth, and which had (and still have) a complex and frequently embattled relationship with sexuality. We will examine the way sex and religion *compete* for the same neural networks as a way to understand why sex has been viewed as threatening to many religions, and we survey how particular religions have sought to control sex, as well as analyze those strategies from a neuroscientific point of view.

We will consider, in chapter 4, exceptions to the tendency to regard sexuality as detrimental to human advancement and enlightenment. There are many groups that have found ways of embracing sexuality. For such groups—such as sects of tantric Buddhism, Hinduism's devadasis, Sumer's sacred prostitutes, and Ephesus's Cult of Venus—sexuality is a highly spiritual and sacred activity. The sexual rites, practices, and other manifestations of sacred spirituality and sexuality are regarded by these groups as a path to self-realization and mystical union.

In chapter 5, we will explore the OM practice that combines sexuality and spirituality and find out what happens in the brain during such a practice. We will also begin to explore what happens in our brains when we have a transformational or "enlightenment" type of experience. Is enlightenment or mysticism similar to falling in love? Having an orgasm? The infatuated brain undergoes remarkable changes, which are eventually consolidated (if the infatuation develops) into a new way of processing reality that now includes the beloved. We also compare the neurological contours of religious fervor and the erotic.

While we will initially focus on the parts of the brain involved in this dance between sexuality and spirituality, there is also an underlying biological mechanism involving different neurotransmitters—the molecules that neurons use to talk to each other—which will be covered in chapter 6. Molecules such as dopamine, oxytocin, and others are important players in the relationship between sexuality and spirituality. One of the best examples of this comes from research into the use of hallucinogenic drugs. The neurotransmitter systems that these unique compounds affect are known, so we can look for links between these brain changes and the powerful experiences people have while using psychedelics. Because these psychedelic experiences are so powerful, research into the use of these drugs for the treatment of various mental disorders is exploding. In my own research, I have considered the ways hallucinogens such as Methylenedioxymethamphetamine (MDMA or Ecstasy) and psilocybin affect the brain and help sharpen and expand our understanding of the intimate relationship between sexuality and spirituality. These topics will be covered in chapter 7.

From there, we will explore the light and dark aspects that are part of our sexuality and spirituality. In chapter 8, we find the similarities and differences between sexual and spiritual addictions, especially in the context of how spiritual pursuits can be useful in people with various addictions. Chapter 9 discusses the broader relationship between psychology, sexuality, and religion. We will consider psychological disorders and discuss "normal" and "abnormal" states of the psyche and the spirit. We then explore in chapter 10 how sexuality and religion can be used in ways that lead to negative beliefs and behaviors. This includes various abuses and even atypical beliefs such as cults.

As bad as various abuses, delusions, and cults can be, there is the even more problematic and well-known fact that religion can engage the potentially violent parts of who we are. This topic is explored in chapter 11, as well as profiling what violent brain states look like. The chapter will also delve into the neurobiology of sexual aggression and violence, and its spiritual and religious corollaries. We can begin to develop a map of a sexual-spiritual psychology that revolves around attraction, shame, modesty, jealousy, rejection, idealization, ecstasy, and awe.

Of course, all is not bad or evil when it comes to sexuality and spirituality. In chapter 12, the topics will include how sexuality and mating rituals form the rudimentary building blocks of morals and ethics. The basic ideas of not stealing (especially a mate), connecting with another person, and expressing compassion and empathy are directly derived from mating rituals and sexual mores. These moral codes also lie at the heart of spirituality and religion. In chapter 13, we'll look at how morals can become part of a greater ability of our sexuality and spirituality to foster compassion, empathy, and love within human beings.

Lastly, in chapter 14, we will consider the similarities and differences between genders when it comes to sexuality, and ultimately, spirituality. Perhaps an understanding of these common and positive elements of sexuality and spirituality can propel humanity toward a greater enlightenment by helping us understand the similarities and differences in our shared biology.

This is a book that has been gestating inside me for over 30 years; its impetus goes back to the beginning of my career. When I was a young medical student at the University of Pennsylvania, my mentor was Dr. Eugene (Gene) d'Aquili, a psychiatrist who had also trained as an anthropologist. Gene had a particular interest in brain evolution and design, the nature of ritual, and the origins of religion. A heavyset man with a young, unlined face, he was the most intelligent person I have ever met, fluent in four languages with an encyclopedic mind.

About once a month, my wife and I would dine at his eighteenth-century farmhouse (designed and built by one of his ancestors), sitting around a table comprised of great scientific minds. We ate, drank, and sang as if we were kids around a campfire. The only difference was the conversation, which typically involved questions about brain evolution, mystical experiences, and Gene's absolute favorite topic—rituals. He was particularly fascinated by how mating rituals in animals had carried over in early humans and became religious rituals. He argued that these rituals were the foundation and the great shaper of civilization. Not everyone, of course, agreed with this idea. But it was Gene's house and Gene's table. Gene's book, *Spectrum of Ritual*, had established him as one of the foremost experts on ritual in the world. So, for that topic, even Nobel laureates at the table were loath to battle him on his own turf.

As a young researcher working with Gene, I was fascinated by his idea of how mating rituals had been the basis of the way religions formed, and thus the topic became a prime target of our investigations. However, since mating rituals draw their power from the sexual experience, we recognized that the neurobiology of sex had to be intimately linked with spirituality and religion. At the time, we just didn't know how to demonstrate this directly.

I was training in the field of nuclear medicine, an approach that uses small amounts of radioactive materials to study different organs in the body. These new scanning technologies allowed us to visualize how the brain worked in a variety of neurological and psychiatric disorders, and its potential was quickly realized. If we could use brain scans to study Alzheimer's disease or depression, then it was hypothesized we could use the same technology to study the brain during religious rituals such as meditation or prayer.

Unfortunately, Gene did not live to see the results of our efforts due to his untimely death from a heart attack in 1998. However, I continued on with our work, although the important sexual angle of our investigations admittedly languished. We had plenty of empirical inferences and compelling theories, but we lacked hard data. Fortuitously, years later, as a result of our most recently conducted research into OM, I finally had a way to add meat to the bones of the ideas that had been so important to Gene and me.

The common origin of sexuality and spirituality inside of us is "dimly starred" in the words of poet Wallace Stevens. Nonetheless, it is there. We can feel it. Too often have we been alienated and estranged from that indispensable connection. I hope the rest of this book provides a remedy and points toward a path for growth as a species, while demanding a long overdue reckoning and reconciliation.

PART I

THE FOUNDATION

CHAPTER 1

IN THE BEGINNING....

"What is love?" asks Socrates in [Plato's Symposium]. . . . "He is a great spirit (daimon) and like all spirits he is intermediate between the divine and the mortal. . . . He is the mediator who spans the chasm which divides men and gods, and therefore in him all is bound together. . . ."
—Rollo May, *Love & Will*

CROCODILE LOVE

Flashback one hundred and fifty million years ago, during the late Jurassic. The sky is always cloudy, the humidity dense. In the subtropical swamps of the supercontinent of Gondwana, a male *Machimosaurus rex*, a crocodile the size of a small bus, swims cautiously toward a female of the species. Although *Machimosuarus* are highly aggressive cannibals, eating her is not what he has in mind. He undulates, emitting a low-pitched bellow, repeatedly slapping his massive snout on the murky water in a vigorous display. Glands near his jaw release an oily musk. The female's wide nostrils inhale the scent; her heartbeat and breath quicken. She mimics him, walloping her snout on the water's surface, secreting pungent oils from her genitals to indicate her receptivity. Their snouts touch, and they rub each other's armored backs and heads. He glides away and she follows. He twists and turns; her body mirrors his. It is as if they have found a way to become intimately connected: nothing will distract them from this powerful sexual trance. The ritualistic mating dance extends over several hours. When they are finally ready, they twist tightly around each other, two becoming one. He inserts his penis into her cloaca, and, within minutes, delivers his sperm. After hours of ritualistic foreplay, they have finally done the deed, at last doing their part to produce the next generation of their species.

Why is this mating "ritual" so elaborate? Isn't there a simpler way (wham, bam, thank you ma'am)? The extended display expends valuable energy and makes the crocs vulnerable to predators. Yet this ritual, and all mating rituals, appear to be absolutely essential to identify the correct mate and help the mating pair come together for sex. As a neuroscientist who has studied the brain for three decades, I can tell you that neither of these tasks is as easy and straightforward as it might seem. Through the pages that follow, you will learn why mating rituals are elaborate and explore how they have evolved and grown in complexity during the past 150 million years.

We now shift the scene to the south of France 100,000 years ago. A great ice sheet covers much of Europe. A small group of Neanderthals huddle around a fire at the mouth of a cave, gnawing on the remains of a red deer they have recently killed and subsequently roasted. Nearby, a young adult Neanderthal man cautiously approaches a female. He smiles, puffs out his chest, makes soft sounds, and does his best to indicate to her that he is interested in mating. Her arousal and interest are signaled to him through her dilated eyes and quickening breath, similar to the *Machimosaurus rex*. Across a vast evolutionary terrain, little has changed, although she also shows an excited smile and flushing of the face to indicate her potential interest. Still somewhat uncertain, he registers these signs and reaches for her. They move rhythmically together, sensing each other's pheromones— the smells they emit—which signal that they're sexually ready. When at last they engage in the act, their sex is highly rhythmic. We don't know how long the act itself would have lasted, if she would have climaxed, or what her degree of sexual arousal might have been. We also can't say that arousal was consistent across individuals of that time, or if it depended on a number of factors, as is the case in modern times. However, what we can say is that during sexual excitement our male and female ancestors would have felt a rush of hormones, neurotransmitters like dopamine and oxytocin, and the turning on of the autonomic nervous system—the automated part of the nervous system that connects the brain and body—regulating feelings of arousal and bliss.

It was likely an ecstatic experience that felt more than just physical, embodying the ineffable. So, it is not beyond comprehension why early men and women made these intimate experiences central to their existence and to their beliefs about the universe, eventually connecting sex with subsequent childbirth. As a result, the miraculous and mysterious creation of new human life was undoubtedly viewed as a microcosm of the creation of the world—a creation infused with spiritual significance.

THE MODERN STUDY OF SEXUALITY

Flash forward to Fall 2019. I prepare a pleasant couple in their thirties for the huge brain scanner that I use at the Department of Integrative Medicine at Thomas Jefferson University in the Philadelphia suburbs. The couple is about to perform a unique kind of ritualistic spiritual practice called Orgasmic Meditation or OM (pronounced *ōhm*). The male, fully clothed, carefully positions himself on the floor, sitting next to the female who is lying on a bunch of large pillows and is naked from the waist down. She butterflies her legs open, and they begin a short, largely scripted, preparatory dialogue. Their interaction has a rhythmic quality in both sound and touch. When they are ready, she allows him to stroke her clitoris for exactly fifteen minutes. At a midway point, I administer a radioactive isotope through the intravenous catheter that I inserted into each of them prior to the OM practice. The isotope will capture their brain activity during the practice in a PET scan that we acquire after their practice is over.

When I was first approached about studying OM, I immediately recognized that it might be the missing link, the key to discovering the ancient and intimate relationship in our brain between sexuality and spirituality. The OM practice is supposed to work by ritualistically connecting the two individuals in a repeatable and predictable form, using the stroking of the clitoris as a meditative element. I was tremendously curious to see if the meditative patterns of brain activity, which I had carefully mapped in my prior work, would be reflected in the OM practice, and if primitive brain areas would be more prominent in OM than, say, typical instances of Buddhist, Christian, and Sufi meditation. I knew that if I could scientifically show the tight relationship between sexuality and spirituality in the body and brain that I would have the potential to heal a bitter rift in our culture and psyches.

It is my hope that the OM study and the information that follows in this book will radically change how we think about the relationship between these two powerful aspects of our humanity: sexuality and spirituality. We have been trapped in a kind of perennial childhood, struggling to grow into a maturity that today seems both urgent and elusive. Religion, while espousing lofty goals, has demonstrated again and again its proclivity for rigidity, intolerance, and violent tribalism, while our sexual nature is frequently contorted by prudishness, treated as bestial, or expressed in a manner devoid of love.

But what if we can bridge the great divide that exists in our cultures, our religions, and inside so many of us? What if it was possible to overcome the divide between incarnation and transcendence, body and soul, reason and emotion, intuition and logic, empiricism and the esoteric, the corporeal and ethereal, science and religion, and sexuality and spirituality?

As we come to understand the intricate neurological relationship between religious and sexual feelings and behaviors, we will come to know ourselves in new ways. For many of us, I suspect, this will feel like both a marriage of disparate parts of ourselves, and a personal reclamation—a return to a sense of wholeness that has been lost. A desire for connection and union is so much a part of who we are; impeding or neglecting it squelches our natural response to life. And it is this desire for connection that leads to our sense of spirituality and religion as approaches to fostering this fundamental connection.

THE ORIGINS OF RELIGION

There have been a number of attempts at explaining the origin of religious and spiritual expression in human beings from an evolutionary point of view. Some have suggested that religious beliefs helped to create cohesive societies by providing a sense of morals and a sense of community.[7] This is likely the case as there are no examples of human civilization arising

---

7   Sosis R, Alcorta C. Signaling, solidarity, and the sacred: the evolution of religious behavior. *Evolution Anthropol.* 2003;12(6):264-274.

without some type of religious or spiritual elements being present. For instance, the ten-thousand-year-old temple, Gobekli Tepe, in southeastern Turkey indicates that religious activities preceded organized societies by thousands of years. Even sites such as Stonehenge indicate the importance of various religious or spiritual activities long before cities and towns were formed. Most of the ancient cities of Mesopotamia and Egypt were based around temples with the leaders, such as the Pharaohs, being regarded as Gods.

The organized structure of these societies was almost all based on religious rituals and practices. Thus, the tenets of the religions including birth, death, and leadership rituals suffused these societies and created cohesion among the people. Their rules of business and behavior were also guided by religious beliefs. The Bible and other sacred texts provide a system of morals through such concepts as the Ten Commandments. While there are ten that most people know of, the Bible actually contains a total of 613 commandments, many of which pertain to legal or financial dealings—what to do when someone steals something from another person, like an ox for example—"Whoever steals an ox or a sheep and slaughters it or sells it must pay back five head of cattle for the ox and four sheep for the sheep." (Exodus 22:1 NIV).

Other scholars have discussed the possibility that rather than creating cohesive societies, religion represents a complex "signaling" mechanism to identify people within a group.[8] In this way, the people that follow the same rituals and prayers that you do are part of your group and vice versa. After all, adhering to the tenets of a religion requires a great amount of effort and cost, both in terms of time and resources. It is highly unlikely that you are going to follow religious rules and rituals unless you truly believe in them. So, if you are willing to incur the cost of the religion, it signals that you are part of that group.

Still others have suggested that religion has arisen as a byproduct (or epiphenomenon) of a highly complex brain capable of asking questions

---

8   Boyer P. *Religion Explained*. Basic Books; 2001.

about the nature of reality and solving complex social and scientific problems.[9] If the brain is complex enough to ponder the origin of the universe or why human beings seem so unique among animals, maybe it will also come up with the notion of God. Some prominent scholars have argued that religion is related to a hyperactive agency detection device (HADD) in which we see a mind or consciousness in places that it does not exist, specifically in the whole universe.[10] This does make some sense as we tend to imbue our cars and other inanimate objects with some semblance of a mind or sentience. We even refer to these objects as if they are people—it is common to give names to cars, boats, and even spacecraft. If we expand this concept to think of the entire universe as deriving from consciousness itself, as seen in the Buddhist and Hindu traditions, perhaps it belongs to a being or God.

But given all of these possibilities, one of the critical pieces that I have felt was missing in virtually all of them is that evolution is based upon the ability of an animal to create the next generation of its species. In so doing, animals that pass on their genes end up continuing to survive. The important point of this procreation aspect of evolution is that it comes down to sex. Thus, animals have highly specialized and complex mating behaviors that have developed through millions of years of evolution, presumably to facilitate procreation. It would seem then that any evolutionary model of a given trait must somehow be tied back to mating.

It always made sense to me, therefore, that sex must have something to do with religion and spirituality from an evolutionary perspective. In other words, the reason we have religion should be because of sex, or at least the interrelationship between sex and religion.

One other important point about the process of evolution itself is that there are two main ways in which adaptations guide species development. One mechanism is the well-known "survival of the fittest" concept, or *natural selection*. This aspect of evolution is based on various physical

---

9   Lindenfors P, Svensson J. Evolutionary explanations for religion: an interdisciplinary critical review. *Res Ideas Outcomes.* 2021;7:e66132. doi: 10.3897/rio.7.e66132.

10   Barrett JL. *Cognitive Science, Religion, and Theology: From Human Minds to Divine Minds.* Templeton Press; 2011.

traits that make an animal more prone to procreate or better off to survive, which in turn, makes it more prone to procreate. Being better able to have more offspring might come in the form of producing extra sperm in males so that it makes it more likely for them to impregnate a female. Being better able to survive might relate to running faster, which could be an important survival adaptation because it helps an animal to either outrun their main predator or outrun their main food source. And by being more likely to survive, they are alive long enough to have more opportunities to procreate.

But all traits come with constraints as well. Running fast requires the mechanical ability to move the legs quickly. There are limitations based on the size of the bones and the strength of the muscles, or the amount of food that needs to be eaten to power those muscles. Evolution is a balance between what works best from one adaptive perspective to another. Every trait has the potential to be good and useful or to be bad and destructive. As we will discuss in chapter 11, aggression and violence in humans can be adaptive, but are also destructive, and there is need for the balanced presence of compassion, love, and cohesion, at least within human groups.

The second primary mechanism by which evolution works is *sexual selection*. This has to do with how mates are selected within a given animal species. Sexual selection helps explain many unusual animal characteristics such as large moose antlers or a peacock's bright plumage.[11] These ornaments do not help the animal survive, but rather make the males or females more attractive to the opposite sex. For instance, peahens seem to inherently like bright feathers on their mates. As a result, over time, more male peacocks evolved bright tail feathers. However, large ornaments have sometimes become a hindrance for survival. It is not easy holding up your head with 30-pound antlers on top of them. But, in spite of their bulk, it is believed that these excessive ornaments may signal fitness to a prospective mate, since to have large ornaments comes at a cost for survival. Thus, it is inferred that a moose with big antlers probably is very strong, and hence, physically adaptive for survival.

Some scholars have gone on to argue that the large human brain is adaptive from a physical survival perspective since it helps us solve problems,

---

11   Miller G. *The Mating Mind*. Anchor Books; 2001.

find food, and build shelter—tasks that all lead to enhanced survival. Other scholars have suggested that the large brain might be the result of sexual selection instead.[12] The large brain enabled people to create music, poetry, and humor, all traits that ended up attracting mates to one another. Of course, both males and females would have to evolve large brains together. If a male had a great sense of humor, but the female was too dumb to notice, then mating wouldn't work out very well. As females developed bigger brains and got smarter, males similarly developed bigger brains, and vice versa. Over time, males and females became more attracted to each other through various brain-related processes that contributed to sexual selection.

An important question is whether religion and spirituality in humans is a physically adaptive trait leading to enhanced overall survival, or is a sexually adaptive trait leading to better mating strategies.

The answer that I propose is a resounding, "Yes!" Religion and spirituality probably are doubly adaptive. And that is why, as I wrote in one of my first books, God won't go away.[13] In that book, *Why God Won't Go Away*, my colleagues and I argued that religion maps well onto the two most basic brain processes—self-maintenance and self-transcendence. These broadly defined goals of the brain's functions help us survive physically (self-maintenance) and help us grow through life and make deeper connections to the world around us (self-transcendence). But if religion provides a mechanism for both processes, that means that it helps with physical survival (through maintaining the self) and also with sexual selection (making personal connections).

ONE SIZE DOES NOT FIT ALL

One important point to emphasize here is that we are going to explore many different practices, beliefs, and traditions. And what I have learned

---

12   Miller G. *The Mating Mind*. Anchor Books; 2001.

13   Newberg A, d'Aquili E, Rause V. *Why God Won't Go Away: Brain Science and the Biology of Belief.* Ballantine Books; 2001.

from all of my studies exploring the beliefs and experiences of thousands of individuals, is that there is no "one size fits all" approach. This is true for sexuality as well as spirituality. Each person has their own unique belief system that arises from the sum total of their genetics, gestational development, birth, parents, siblings, personal successes and traumas, friends, teachers, lovers, and ultimately their own life experiences.

If there are eight billion people in the world, then there are eight billion religions. Each person looks at religion and spirituality from their own unique view even if they share many similar elements with a group of people.

Similarly, sexuality is universal, but some feel it more and some feel it less. People are turned on by potential mates of all varieties of intelligence, emotions, sizes, colors, scents, and many other attributes.[14] Some are turned on by the same gender, some by other genders, some by both. With this incredible variety, we will be able to consider where some universals can be found, but there will almost always be some exception to the rule. Almost all birds fly, but penguins swim. Almost all mammals give birth to live offspring, but platypuses lay eggs.

As we explore the impact of sexuality on spirituality, we will seek to find universals, but always recognize that there are unique characteristics to everyone's view of reality and everyone's belief systems.

We will discuss all of this in more detail in the pages that follow. Suffice it to say here that this book hopes to connect some of my earliest research on the evolutionary processes associated with brain functions that support religious practices and experiences with the most recent brain scan studies my colleagues and I have performed. The results help to demonstrate the profound and deep link between our brain, sexuality, and spirituality.

---

14   Buss DM. *The Evolution of Desire: Strategies of Human Mating.* Basic Books, 2016.

CHAPTER 2

RHYTHMS AND RITUALS:

WHAT'S A NICE GIRL LIKE YOU DOING IN A PLACE LIKE THIS?

Ritual is the passage way of the soul into the infinite.

—Algernon Blackwood

Religious rituals have occurred, in virtually every human culture, with an almost infinite variety of form. But in every known case, a singular principle holds true: When religious ritual is effective, it inclines the brain to adjust its cognitive and emotional perceptions of the self in a way that religiously-minded persons interpret as a closing of the distance between the self and God.

—Newberg, d'Aquili, and Rause

THE BEGINNINGS OF RITUALS

There is no question that animal rituals have a powerful effect on their brain and body. These rituals enable two animals that do not typically come close together to identify a potential mate and enable the sexual act to begin. The spatial, emotional, and sexual parts of the brain all play a role in this dance with the goal of producing the next generation of the species. Human beings evolved from these animals, and our rituals have come along for the ride. Human beings are as affected, if not more affected, by rituals than almost any other animal on the planet. In fact, we have developed rituals for nearly every aspect of life.

We have life cycle rituals—birth, growing up, leaving home, marriage, and death rituals. We have rituals for getting up in the morning, going to work, setting up your desk, coming home, making dinner, and going to sleep. Virtually every human institution has rituals. Schools, businesses, sports teams, and governments are all loaded with rituals. And of course, some of the most prominent examples of rituals come in the form of religious and spiritual rituals.

Where do all of these rituals come from? The simple answer is sex. If you look at virtually every animal species from insects to reptiles to mammals, animal rituals are mating rituals. They have been built into the physiology of virtually every animal on our planet in order to allow sex to occur. The body movements, vocalizations, visual displays, smells, and all sorts of rhythmic activity drive the autonomic nervous system to experience a profound sense of connection with another animal. Sex and mating rituals are what helped all of these mechanisms get into our brain and body in the first place. From there, all other rituals came about. In the end, all rituals do one main thing: they connect us to the world and each other in powerful ways. It is that sense of connection which is fundamental to all rituals, and particularly religious and spiritual rituals. Remember, the basis of mating rituals is to connect two animals together to create the next generation. Through various senses and rhythms, the brain is driven to lower our personal boundaries enough so that we might connect with something else—preferably an appropriate mate.

Human beings are no different from any other animal in this regard. Through our senses and various rhythmic activities, our brain and body feel a sense of connection with "something else." When it comes to mating, that something else is another human being. That is how a male knows the answer to the question, "What's a nice girl like you doing in a place like this?" She is looking for someone whose rhythms resonate with her.

There is no single way in which this works. It is a matter of finding the rhythmic key to the ritualistic lock.

But beyond that, the "something else" can be a group of human beings, a society, a country, the whole of humanity, or something even greater.[15]

---

15   d'Aquili EG, Newberg AB. *The Mystical Mind: Probing the Biology of Religious Experience.* Fortress Press; 1999.

Through rituals, we may have intense experiences of connection with the universe, God, or ultimate reality. These latter experiences are typically described in the mystical literature of the great religious traditions. For now, it is enough to know that it is not a stretch to go from basic mating rituals to a discussion about profound mystical experiences. But let us take this journey a bit slower. Let us start by considering how human rituals started as mating rituals and then became part of religious and spiritual worship.

MATING IN HUMANS

As with other animals, humans use a variety of sensations and rhythms during the mating process. Typically, these involve dances, parties, or other events that are filled with rhythmic sounds, flashing lights, and an assortment of smells and tastes. Nearly every available sense is called upon to be part of the action. From the taste of alcohol to the smell of sweat to the rhythmic gyrations of someone's hips, a great deal of possibility exists to be turned on by the rituals. Of course, not every culture has the same rituals, but they ultimately all require rhythms of some type to get two people together.

The notion of being "turned on" is an interesting one. Research indicates that this is exactly what happens in the brain during sexual arousal—it literally turns on. Brain scan studies of sexual arousal through visual pornography show many parts of the brain turning on or becoming more active. And brain scan studies of sexual stimulation of both male and female genitals showed even greater increased activity in a variety of brain areas including those associated with emotions and sensations.[16]

Specific rhythms, particularly those with a rapid beat, activate the autonomic nervous system's sympathetic, or arousal, side. The autonomic nervous system actually consists of two primary components: the sympathetic

---

16   Georgiadis JR, Kortekaas R, Kuipers R, et al. Regional cerebral blood flow changes associated with clitorally induced orgasm in healthy women. *Eur J Neurosci.* 2006;24(11):3305-16.

or arousal side and the parasympathetic or quiescent side.[17] The arousal side turns on when we are excited either positively or negatively. It is the neurological basis for the fight, flight, freeze, or fawn response which increases heart rate and blood pressure, dilates the eyes, and expends the body's energy stores in readiness for action. The quiescent side turns on when we are trying to relax and rejuvenate our energy supplies. It reduces heart rate and blood pressure, activates digestion, and prepares us for sleep.

Evolutionarily speaking, the autonomic nervous system is one of the oldest parts of our brain and body. Evidence of an autonomic nervous system is present in nearly all vertebrates (animals with spinal cords) for the past 450 million years, and the rudiments of this system go back even further into some invertebrate animals. It is regulated by a similarly ancient structure called the hypothalamus which sits right on top of the brain stem. Although only about an inch in size, the hypothalamus is the primary controller of the entire body. It regulates the autonomic nervous system's arousal and quiescent arms but also controls virtually all of our hormone systems including our sex hormones. In this way, the hypothalamus regulates our flight, fight, freeze, or fawn response, our sex hormone cycles including menstruation and puberty, and, of course, mating.

Not surprisingly, during sexual excitement, we literally (and physiologically) become aroused, with an increase in our heart rate, blood pressure, dilated eyes, and sweaty palms. Of course, it is hoped that this stimulation of our own body resonates with a similar stimulation in another person's body. When the rhythms of both bodies come together in a resonance, the self-other dichotomy is broken down and the two can begin to connect.

The notion of resonance is not just metaphorical. Research studies have shown that the brains of people in intimate connection with each other actually respond in reciprocal ways. They literally resonate with each other. For example, a study performed at the Social Brain Laboratory in the Netherlands showed that when people play charades, and connect with the correct answer, they activate similar areas in both the sender's and receiver's

---

17   Newberg AB. *Neurotheology: How Science Can Enlighten Us About Spirituality*. Columbia University Press; 2018.

brains, especially in the areas involved in language production and recep-
tion.[18]

Researchers at Princeton University studied pairs of individuals communicating with each other in a Functional Magnetic Resonance Imaging
(fMRI) scanner and found that neuronal resonance appears when participants communicate effectively and disappears when participants communicate poorly. In fact, they could even predict the degree of successful
communication by determining how closely their brains resonated with
each other.[19]

If the rhythms and rituals lead to sexual activity, this sense of arousal
continues. Various hormones get in on the act as well. Testosterone in men
and estrogen in women will further increase the sense of arousal. And as
climax or orgasm occurs, both the arousal and quiescent parts of the autonomic nervous system kick in and we feel a rush of energy and strong sense
of bliss almost at the same time. If this sounds at all familiar with spiritual
experiences, it should. Spiritual experiences are typically associated with
both strong feelings of arousal and awareness, along with profound feelings
of bliss. But we will discuss this important combination a bit more in the
next chapter.

Modern studies of sexual arousal and sexual climax, particularly with
brain imaging, are not simple studies to perform. Typically, a person is either sexually stimulated by another, or self-stimulated through masturbation, while having their brain scanned. You can imagine how challenging
this must be for both the investigator and the research subject. An MRI
machine is not a particularly erotic and playful place to be. But fortunately,
the human brain is so overly sexual in general, that by showing some basic
pornographic videos, and stimulating the genitals, many people can still
achieve orgasm no matter how much they are poked and prodded.

---

18   Stephens GJ, Silbert LJ, Hasson U. Speaker-listener neural coupling underlies successful
      communication. *Proc Natl Acad Sci U S A*. 2010;107(32):14425-30.

19   Schippers MB, Gazzola V, Goebel R, Keysers C. Playing charades in the fMRI: are
      mirror and/or mentalizing areas involved in gestural communication? *PLoS One*.
      2009;4(8):e6801. doi:10.1371/journal.pone.0006801.

OM AND THE AUTONOMIC NERVOUS SYSTEM

In the context of our OM study, we will talk later about the brain scans we acquired showing the many changes associated with the OM practice; for now it is important to mention that we also measured changes in the body, particularly with regard to the autonomic nervous system. Just as with typical sexual stimulation, the people engaging in OM reported experiencing an intense sense of arousal during the practice. This is an important point. While some meditation practices are designed to help people relax, many are dedicated to inducing a profound sense of arousal and concentration. This is, in fact, the goal of the OM practice. The mind is not quiet, but is intently focused on the sexual stimulation itself. Two of our study participants described their experiences:

> I feel electricity in my finger. Heat in my chest and face. I have felt deep connection with the other person. Loss of self and a sense of bliss as if my skin has melted and felt a union with everything. —Male participant

> I can feel a current of electricity from my partner's finger to my clitoris and it radiates throughout my entire body. There is a stillness and a calm that comes over me, a feeling of sinking deeper into myself and into my body. . . . I feel like my normal awareness of the room, of my physical body will disappear and I will be a rocking, pulsing movement of energy shifting back and forth, ebbing and flowing.—Female participant

This latter quote is of particular interest since it speaks to the push and pull of various feelings of energy and relaxation during the OM practice. For the most part, this happens in sexual activity and mating as well. It is not all "Go! Go! Go!" It is important to allow for both active and passive elements. That is what creates the rhythm that drives the ritual and leads to ecstasy.

Most meditation and spiritual practices are quite similar. If you have ever done an intense meditation retreat, you will know that it can be as exhausting as it can be relaxing. Intense meditation can be quite difficult due to the persistent need to pay attention during the practice. It requires a hyperarousal state to maintain that focus, but then there are times when it can feel like a hyperblissful experience as well. In a similar manner, the OM practice requires a great deal of attention by both the giver (or stroker in OM lingo) and receiver (the strokee). The receiver has to pay attention to the stimulation of her clitoris. But the giver must pay attention to the receiver to make sure that the manual stimulation is being done in such a way that facilitates the practice effectively.

There is a great deal of reciprocal interaction between both participants during the practice, accompanied by an intense sense of arousal for both individuals. This is exactly what we saw in our OM research study. Both males and females had significantly increased heart rate measures during the OM practice. Their sympathetic or arousal system in their brain and body was turned on. Importantly, this connects the sexual part of the OM practice to the spiritual, or meditative, part. There is a hyperarousal state that occurs during both OM and intense spiritual practices. Interestingly, after the OM session, as the heart rate dropped, the heart rate variability increased above the baseline levels, particularly in the women. This suggests that not only is there a profound sense of arousal during the practice, but that as the result of doing the practice, the aftereffect is a sense of calm or blissfulness. This too is reported in many meditative practices: a combination of arousal and blissfulness.

You might think that this is also similar to sexual climax since many people, particularly men, get quite drowsy after sex. However, the difference with OM is that climax is not the goal, and usually does not occur. Thus, the responses we see in OM indicate a more spiritual side of the practice rather than a sexual one. But it is important that sexual arousal, as well as the relaxation that occurs after the act of sex, seem to overlap with meditation.

From an evolutionary perspective, this physiological effect is critical. It is essential that sex feels good, otherwise animals won't do it. The arousal feels good, but only to a point. The animal has to be encouraged to complete the sexual act, and thus, climax must feel even better. That powerful sense of blissfulness right after intense arousal does the trick. The same holds true for spiritual activity.

During previous work with Gene d'Aquili, we looked into the complex interactions of the autonomic nervous system. Typically, one side or the other becomes activated at any given time. This makes sense as we would not want our quiescent side to turn on when we are caught in a burning building, and we would not want our arousal side to kick in when we are trying to go to sleep for the night. Although typically only one side of the autonomic nervous system turns on at a time, there is growing evidence that they sometimes can turn on together, particularly when one side is turned on to a very high degree.[20]

With these complex relationships in mind, we previously proposed five different states of autonomic activity that are associated with spiritual experiences.[21] Other scholars, early on, also noted the importance of both arms of the autonomic nervous system when it comes to spiritual practices.[22] The five states of autonomic activity we proposed and observed are:

Hyperarousal – Associated with intense feelings of arousal or energy

Hyperquiescent – Associated with a profound sense of bliss and relaxation

Hyperarousal with Quiescent Breakthrough – Associated with a sense of calm superimposed on intense feelings of arousal or energy

Hyperquiescent with Arousal Breakthrough – Associated with a sense of arousal or energy superimposed on a profound sense of bliss and relaxation

Hyperquiescent with Hyperarousal – Associated with a combination of intense feelings of energy and bliss

---

20 Weissman DG, Mendes WB. Correlation of sympathetic and parasympathetic nervous system activity during rest and acute stress tasks. *Int J Psychophysiol*. 2021;162:60-68.

21 d'Aquili EG, Newberg AB. *The Mystical Mind: Probing the Biology of Religious Experience*. Fortress Press; 1999.

22 Peng CK, Mietus JE, Liu Y, et al. Exaggerated heart rate oscillations during two meditation techniques. *Int J Cardiol*. 1999;70(2):101-107; Gellhorn E, Kiely WF. Mystical states of consciousness: neurophysiological and clinical aspects. *J Nerv Mental Dis*. 1972; 154:399-405.

Let us explore these in more detail so you can see the complex inter-actions that arise and how they are related to various aspects of spiritual experience. While doing so, keep in mind that the autonomic nervous system was designed in large part for mating to occur. As mentioned, the autonomic nervous system has an arousal and quiescent side—scientifically called the sympathetic and parasympathetic systems—that connects to vir-tually every organ in the body telling them to get ready for action or to settle down and rejuvenate. But what do we experience if either one of these systems becomes activated to a heightened state?

In the OM practice, our data suggest that the arousal system is turned on to a very high degree. This hyperarousal state is experienced as a pro-found sense of energy, alertness, and power throughout the body—what our participants referred to above as *electricity*. Such states are also found in other circumstances. For example, flow states in which a person feels like an immense amount of sensory information is flowing seamlessly through them is another type of hyperarousal state.[23] This state is described by fighter jet pilots or during extreme athletic activities such as surfing.[24] Various intense religious practices such as charismatic Christian services can also produce a similar experience with all of the participants swaying, dancing, and singing in a very excited manner.

A second possible autonomic state is one of hyperquiescence in which the parasympathetic nervous system is turned on to a very high degree. One might expect such a state to feel tranquil or blissful as when one is listening to slow chanting or performing a very calm breathing meditation. The whole body and mind feels calm, and when connected with a spiritual concept, the world can feel a relaxing place. Studies have shown that such practices, even when they evoke mild increases in the quiescent system, lead

---

23   Csikszentmihalyi M. *Flow: The Psychology of Optimal Experience*. Harper and Row; 1990.; Kozhevnikov M, Li Y, Wong S, Obana T, Amihai I. Do enhanced states exist? boosting cognitive capacities through an action video-game. *Cognition*. 2018;173:93-105.

24   Ibid.; Chavez, Edward J. Flow in sport: a study of college athletes. *Imagination, Cognition and Personality*. 2008;28(1): 69–91.

to reductions in heart rate and blood pressure.[25] Clinically, some people feel that these practices can be useful for patients with high blood pressure or at risk for a heart attack or stroke. But for our purposes, the turning on of the brain's "bliss machine" yields important and common types of meditative or spiritual experiences.

Although either one of the sides of the autonomic nervous system can be turned on to a great extent, there is a fascinating and complex possibility that can happen next. The other side of the autonomic nervous system can turn on at the same time. We used to refer to this as a kind of "breakthrough" phenomenon in which the arousal system can turn on in the midst of a hyperquiescent state, or the quiescent system can turn on in the midst of a hyperarousal state. Let us look at these two options in the context of OM and the context of spiritual experiences.

We discussed that at the end of the OM practice, there is a relatively dramatic sense of calmness that comes over both the giver and the receiver. This is a common effect in intense, hyperarousal states associated with other spiritual practices. Common examples include Sufi dancing or speaking in tongues, the latter which we also studied. During the intense sensations and emotions of the practice, the quiescent part of the autonomic nervous system kicks in and produces an intense feeling of blissfulness. In the moment, it is not uncommon for people to fall to their knees or collapse while experiencing this blissful state.

On the other hand, during a state of hyperquiescence, such as during deep and slow meditation, the arousal side can kick in and produce a sudden experience of arousal and energy. These intrusions of the arousal side of the autonomic nervous system can happen spontaneously or can be evoked by the sound of a bell or gong, or by the use of an image such as Jesus on the cross. As with the experience above, having both arms of the autonomic nervous system turn on at the same time for brief periods can lead to profound experiences that affect other parts of the brain.

---

25   Park SH, Han KS. Blood pressure response to meditation and yoga: a systematic review and meta-analysis. *J Altern Complement Med.* 2017;23(9):685-695; Khandekar JS, Vasavi VL, Singh VP, Samuel SR, Sudhan SG, Khandelwal B. Effect of yoga on blood pressure in prehypertension: a systematic review and meta-analysis. *Scientific World J.* 2021;2021:4039364. doi:10.1155/2021/4039364.

RELIGIOUS RITUALS AND HOW WE SEE THE WORLD

With the various autonomic states in mind, it is possible to see more clearly how the body's sexual physiology helps us to have spiritual experiences. But while the autonomic nervous system is important, it is really the rhythmic stimuli of various rituals that drive the entire system. Religious rituals are particularly good at doing this, as they have co-opted the ritualistic brain that was originally designed for sexual mating. After all, the autonomic nervous system needs help becoming activated.

In the prior chapter, we talked about how animals get "turned on" sexually. While rhythm is important, the various ornaments and callings of animals are the sensory stimuli that drive the system. This occurs in large part through activity in the limbic system, the primary emotional areas of the brain (which includes the amygdala and hippocampus structures that help provide a wide array of emotional responses from joy and happiness to envy, fear, and hatred). The peahen is turned on by bright plumage. Lions are turned on by loud purring sounds. The musky smell of a female elk will drive a male elk crazy. Even insects are turned on by the observation of certain body movements or flight patterns. How does this happen?

Sensory stimuli, after being perceived through the sensory areas of the brain, activate the emotional centers. Thus, bright colors or certain sounds make the animal feel good.

Several years ago, we did a brain scan study of visual religious symbols, and we found how powerful such stimuli can be. We showed people various symbols that were either religious or nonreligious and either positive or negative in terms of emotional content. For example, a positive religious symbol was a heart or a dove. A negative religious symbol was a snake or the face of the devil. A positive nonreligious symbol was a smiley face, while a negative nonreligious symbol was a gun. What we found is that religious symbols had a stronger impact on the primary visual system of the brain. This means that even before we know what the stimulus is, it is having a direct impact on the brain. But we also correlated the person's beliefs with their response to the visual symbols and found that their beliefs shape how these primary sensory areas respond to the visual symbols. People who had more positively emotional beliefs about religion had their primary visual system react to the emotional content differently than those people who held more negatively emotional beliefs. This means that our beliefs directly affect how our brain perceives reality, even at the most basic level. That is why if you believe in one religion or another, or adhere to one political party or another, you perceive everything from that personal perspective from the get-go. Your beliefs make it difficult, if not impossible, to see things from another perspective because they literally alter the way your brain perceives reality in the first place!

This is a crucial concept in all of our research about religious and spiritual beliefs. Our beliefs shape how our brain receives information from the outside world. Our beliefs also form the biases that we use to process that information into our perception of reality. If we believe in God, we can see God all around us; if we do not believe in God, we never see God anywhere. But the same is true of all beliefs, even scientific ones. Scientific paradigms are challenging to change because scientists, who also have human brains, see all of the data from their own vantage point. As genius as Albert Einstein was, he never liked quantum mechanics because his prevailing beliefs about how the universe works led him to the conclusion that quantum mechanics simply did not make sense. He tried in every way he could to disprove quantum mechanics, but each time, new research showed that quantum mechanics looked right. In the end, he never accepted it. We see this in every scientific endeavor from physicists to physicians—and that is because of how our brain works.

THE EVOLUTION OF RITUALS—FROM MATING TO MASS

When it comes to our perception of reality, it is not just a matter of turning on sensory neurons or belief neurons of the brain. We need to connect our perceptions with our emotions and our cognitive processes. To do this requires the release of a variety of neurotransmitters that activate the brain in specific ways. When neurotransmitters such as serotonin or dopamine are released, they can make us feel good when we are stimulated in the right way. And from these positive responses, we create our thoughts and beliefs. Thus, it is no coincidence that rituals have evolved to be particularly good at stimulating us the correct way and helping us form the ways in which we understand the world around us.

It should be no surprise that religious rituals throughout the world, and throughout history, have used a wide array of sensory stimuli to induce powerful changes in the brain. Pick your favorite religion, or any religion for that matter, and think about the visual, auditory, and olfactory stimuli that are used during associated rituals. A church, mosque, or synagogue share so many similar sensory qualities. For instance, there are the visual images of the Star of David, Jesus on the cross, or the letters spelling out key phrases from the Quran, each of which are likely to evoke strong emotional responses. The sacred places also each have a unique smell, perhaps of incense, or of the building materials, or maybe from the bodies of the congregants. And then there are the unique sounds, such as those present from various prayers, instruments, or even echoes off cavernous walls.

Each of these sensory stimuli evoke powerful emotional responses, and when we have such a response, it turns on the limbic system and the autonomic nervous system. As a result, we feel the emotions in our mind and our body. But the limbic system is also connected with our memory system. We want to remember things that are emotionally important to us. Thus, when we perceive certain religious stimuli, we remember what they mean, and in turn, they produce new memories or strengthen old ones. That is why the beliefs of various religious and spiritual traditions become so embedded in the brain.

The rituals and associated stimuli induce powerful emotions which consequently induce powerful beliefs through a complex network of brain structures and functions.

This point should not be understated. Rituals are vitally important because they produce intense memories. Our brain is set up to remember things that impact us emotionally. This makes sense since we want to remember things that are emotionally important or salient to us. It is typical to remember our birthday or anniversary because they are strongly and positively emotional. We also remember the restaurant in which we got food poisoning because it was associated with a very intense negative emotion. Not only are emotions involved, but since the rituals also affect many components of the body, via the autonomic nervous system, we don't just think our beliefs, we feel them throughout the body. It is for precisely this reason that rituals are so important.

But remember that rituals arose from animal mating rituals, which are as much about creating a feeling of arousal as they are about correctly identifying a potential mate. We need to remember fundamentally what animals are part of our species and our group. We recognize the color of the feathers, the shape of the shoulders, or the sound of the vocalization. These sexual identifiers are deeply embedded within us and our memories. If you extrapolate this to religions, the prayers, hymns, and symbols of a particular tradition help identify that tradition. Jews recognize the Star of David while Christians respond to the cross. These identifiers connect the person to the group in intense ways. And from there, in the human brain, more elaborate memories and beliefs could develop.

As the human brain evolved larger and more complex cortical areas and networks that allow for all types of beliefs, cognitions, and ideas, rituals connected into the higher areas. These neurons in these higher areas of the brain that support our beliefs, memories, and abstract thought processes have a particularly important way in which they work that also ties directly into rituals. There is a saying that "neurons that fire together, wire together." There is a physiological truth to this statement. The more a given set or network of neurons function together, the stronger their connections become. This happens on the neuronal level as a set of cells called "interneurons" provide the "glue" to make the connections strong. The more you repeat anything, the stronger those neuronal connections become. This is why successful rituals are based on repetition. The more you sing a hymn or take communion, the more you read a sacred text, or the more you sing the national anthem, the stronger the neuronal connections that support these ideas become.

Rituals can also become more complex as the brain that performs them becomes more complex. But in the end, no matter how complex the brain becomes, it still responds powerfully to sensory stimuli when delivered in the form of rituals, whether they are sexual or spiritual.

Permit me one more observation from everything we have discussed so far about rituals: our data points to a continuum of effects or experiences. This is important since there is such a wide variety of religious and spiritual experiences. Some are very mild, arising simply by walking into a temple, church, mosque, or synagogue. Other experiences are more intense, occurring during specific rituals or festivals such as during Yom Kippur, Easter, or Ramadan. Still others become highly intense, such as mystical or enlightenment experiences. But as we proceed through this experiential continuum, we might expect a continuum of neurological changes from mild to extreme. Sexuality has a similar continuum, ranging from a mild sense of arousal from seeing a sexy movie star or attractive person pass you by to the ecstasy achieved during sexual climax.

It is important to realize that all of these varieties of experiences have value and contribute to the beliefs and behaviors of human beings throughout the world. Thus, while we might think that sexuality is pretty straight forward, it can be quite multifaceted and nuanced across individuals and cultures. Similarly, religious and spiritual rituals are not just a simplistic turning on of the autonomic nervous system, but incorporate all of our emotions, senses, and thoughts. These rituals—in fact all rituals—are quite complex across individuals and cultures, and they have come to embody the various stories and myths of humanity.

CHAPTER 3

MYTHS AND SEXUALITY

A mythological order is a system of images that gives consciousness a sense of meaning in existence, which, my dear friend, has no meaning—it simply is. . . . That's the first function of a mythology, to evoke in the individual a sense of grateful, affirmative awe before the monstrous mystery that is existence.

—Joseph Campbell, *Pathways to Bliss*

WHERE DO MYTHS COME FROM?

The link between rituals and the brain shows how intricately involved sexuality and spirituality find themselves. The biology of mating rituals is something that has to be deeply tied to the evolution of the brain so that sexual reproduction can occur, and so subsequent generations can be born. But the use of rituals for sex is quite simplistic. It makes sense that most animals other than human beings will have rituals that simply begin and end with the mating process. The rituals help identify another member of their species, help two potential mates assess each other, decide if mating should occur, and then enable the mating to occur. Once the mating process is complete, from a sexual perspective, there is no additional action that is now required, and the ritual typically ends. However, the next time rituals take place is during pregnancy, followed by birth, since it is important to establish a connection between the parents (at least the mother) and the infant to help it survive. It turns out that evolution tries to be relatively efficient in how it uses rituals.

In humans, though, rituals are much more complex, not only because of the elements that make them up such as the sensory stimuli, rhythmic behaviors, and intense experiences, but because of the myths that they embody. What exactly is meant by the term *myths*? In everyday language, the term *myth* has developed a pejorative connotation. Myths usually refer to things that are false. Hence, we hear about the "myths of dieting" or even the "myths of sex." The implication is that whatever is being told as part of these myths is a falsehood. It is a myth that you can eat all you want and still lose weight. Similarly, it is a myth that real life sex is just like pornography.

But in the academic and anthropological setting, the concept of myths is much more subtle and nuanced, and not necessarily tantamount to falsehood. In anthropology, myths refer to deep and profound stories that a given group of people or culture develop to help them understand the world around them and how they are to interact within their culture. The most common myths arise out of religious and spiritual belief systems. For example, we know of Greek mythology's incredible stories of the gods that helped the Greeks understand the basis of the universe and various concepts about morality and life itself. Homer's story of Odysseus, king of Ithaca, and his 10-year journey home after the Trojan War similarly demonstrates the power of conviction that can lead one to great success in life. Numerous myths teach us about problems like jealousy and devious behavior, and also the virtues, such as forgiveness or steadfast devotion.

Where did these myths come from? My late colleague, Gene d'Aquili, and I explored the idea that myths derive from the many cognitive processes of the human brain. In the brain, we have networks of structures that function to provide us with the ability to think along many different processing lines. For example, the brain can help us find or apply a sense of causality in the world: we strive to understand what causes what to happen. For the ancients, they wanted to understand the cause of the seasons or the floods. Another important cognitive process provides us with a sense of the holistic character of the world. The parts of our brain that help us with developing a holistic understanding of the universe, primarily involving the parietal and temporal lobes, also enable us to understand how all things are connected. The mythic stories of the monotheistic traditions with a singular God of all things likely derive from this holistic process.

There are also some intriguing cognitive processes that crop up in the mythic stories of humanity, such as the quantitative process. Our brains have a remarkable ability to count numbers and to think mathematically.

Mathematics can be helpful in modern times for knowing how to calculate the cost of various items for sale, and in the ancient world, was used architecturally to build the pyramids and other great structures. But we also have the ability to comprehend numbers as having inherent meaning. In this way, certain numbers are imbued with great power. We see in the Bible numbers such as 3, 10, or 40 in many of the stories: It rained for 40 days and 40 nights, the Hebrews wandered in the desert for 40 years, there are 10 commandments. Odysseus fought the Trojan war for 10 years and then his journey home took another 10 years. These are not just random numbers, but numbers that have great meaning, adding meaning to the sacred nature of the stories.

Thus, the myths themselves, and their content, tend to come from various cognitive and abstract processes of the brain such as the holistic, causal, or quantitative processes. But why do we make these mythic stories in the first place? In some sense it also comes down not so much to the specific cognitive processes of the brain, but to how the brain inherently works on its own, especially to help us survive. Gene d'Aquili and I used to talk about a *cognitive imperative*, which implied that our brain tends to work, whether we want it to or not. For example, if you find yourself in the woods, and you hear the snap of a twig, you don't have to tell your brain to start thinking about what that might be. Your brain automatically starts processing information and provides a story for you to figure out how you should behave. If your brain generates the story that the snap of a twig was a bear, your autonomic nervous system kicks in and you run. If your brain tells you the twig snap might be a bird or a rabbit, you might move toward the sound in the hopes of finding something to eat.

The important point is that the brain operates in an automatic fashion in an effort to produce stories about our surrounding world to help us understand and survive it. On a more profound, philosophical level, as well as a neuroscientific one, our brain has no choice but to create stories about the world around us. From the neuroscientific perspective, we are trapped within our brain, looking out on the world and trying to understand it.[26]

---

26   Newberg AB. *Neurotheology: How Science Can Enlighten Us About Spirituality.* Columbia University Press; 2018.

Every piece of information we have ever come to know about the world enters our consciousness through the processes of our brain. Since we are effectively trapped within our brain, we never truly know if what we think on the inside is accurate with what is present or occurring on the outside. Thus, all of our beliefs are necessarily stories that help us make sense about the world.

In this way, religious and spiritual myths help to tell us something about the origins of the world, whether there is a sacred being who guides the world, and how we are to act morally in order to be the best person we can be. But there are many other myths that have similar qualities. There are stories about how we should act as students in school—paying attention to the teacher, doing our homework, and trying to learn as much as we can. Of course, not all individuals and cultures look at education the same way, and hence, not all education myths are the same. There are political myths, such as whether one should seek a more capitalistic society or a more communistic society. The stories are based on how the brain thinks about the world and other people in the world, and what it sees as the primary ways in which the world operates.

Based on this understanding of myth, even science is a myth. It tells a story about the universe. However, science operates a little differently than most myths since it relies on empirical data and the testing of hypotheses, but it is based on certain foundational concepts that are taken for granted without necessarily being the absolute way of understanding the world. For example, science proceeds based on the notion that the universe can reveal itself through experimentation. Science also generally assumes that the entire physical world is all there is and that there is nothing that is "supernatural." On one hand this makes sense since science itself can't evaluate something that is supernatural. But perhaps science closes itself off to things that exist simply because they can't be observed scientifically.

NEUROTHEOLOGY AND THE STUDY OF MYTH

The potential limitations of science that derive from its own mythic story about the universe is part of the reason why I have pursued a hybrid field called *Neurotheology* over the past 30 years of my career.[27] Much of what you are hearing about in this book derives from a neurotheological perspective.

Neurotheology is the field of study that seeks to understand the relationship between the brain and religious and spiritual phenomena. There are a few important points about neurotheology worth mentioning as we continue to consider the relationship between sexuality and spirituality. If neurotheology is the study of the relationship between the brain and religious phenomena, it is important to realize that that relationship is really a two-way street.[28] Science can certainly tell us a lot about religion and spirituality, but religion and spirituality can tell us something about science as well. Many challenging areas in cosmology and quantum mechanics have elements that seem quite mystical, bordering on spiritual.

As Albert Einstein once proclaimed, "Science without religion is lame, religion without science is blind."[29] I would agree and have always argued that science by itself, while an outstanding approach for understanding the natural world, has certain limitations, particularly when it comes to human experience and consciousness. On the other hand, spirituality can provide important information about who we are as human beings and how we might be connected to something greater. But spirituality and religion often struggle with the way the physical world appears to function. Historically, the Catholic Church treated Galileo terribly when he tried to espouse a new way of looking at the world that was counter to religious precepts, a view that removed the Earth from its location in the center of the universe. Because of these ideas, he was tried and found guilty of heresy. His book was banned, and he was sentenced to house arrest, which lasted until his death in 1642. Fortunately, he was finally forgiven by the Church and cleared of any wrongdoing. Unfortunately, it did not happen until 1992!

---

27   Newberg AB. *Principles of Neurotheology.* Ashgate Publishing Ltd; 2010.

28   Newberg AB. *Neurotheology: How Science Can Enlighten Us About Spirituality.* Columbia University Press; 2018.

29   Einstein A. Science and religion. In: *Ideas and Opinions.* Crown Publishing; 1956.

Hopefully, neurotheology can provide a middle ground by which we can utilize the best of what science and spirituality has to offer to better understand ourselves and our relationship to the world. In the discussion of myth, we have already seen how the brain can help us to generate various elements of these important stories of humanity. Our brain has certain ways of processing information that can lead to the specific elements of a given myth. However, there is a more fundamental philosophical problem that appears to transcend even science, that has to do with how our consciousness experiences the world. It is interesting that in some of the most profound, mystical experiences, as we will consider later, the individual perceives to get beyond the subjective and objective nature of the universe. While this concept is certainly hard to understand for anyone who has not had such an experience, it opens up an entire realm of discussion about what these experiences actually mean and what they represent. For the individual, they feel as if they have touched some fundamental nature of reality that is beyond science and beyond consciousness. Our research has shown that there are physiological processes associated with such experiences, but such findings do not necessarily illuminate what these experiences actually represent in terms of the true nature of reality. That requires much more work in neurotheology, science, and philosophy. It is an epistemological question, the big question, about what reality is and how we can know it.

Neurotheology challenges us to continue asking questions in an attempt to better elucidate the nature of human spirituality and religion, particularly from a brain-related perspective. When it comes to myth making, we can understand the various elements that make up myths as they pertain to the different brain processes. We can also encounter the inherent myth making process of the brain. But we should also ask, "How did all of this get into the brain in the first place?"

SEXUAL SELECTION AND MYTH

The previous discussion shows us how myths can form, as well as the content that they may hold. But from an evolutionary perspective, we might find the same answers for the reasons that religion and ritual got into the brain in the first place—that sex has something to do with our inherent ability to create stories.

In many ways, this is a central argument in the book by Geoffrey Miller, *The Mating Mind*.[30] He states essentially that it is through the process of sexual selection that the human brain evolved to be so complex and so big. Instead of various physical ornaments that other animals found attractive, it turns out that male and female human beings started to find mental attributes more attractive. In this way, the stories that were told by both males and females showcased these mental attributes and helped to bring them together in a way that fostered the ritual connection for mating. The better the story, the better the connection. And religious and spiritual stories are apparently pretty good. After all, some have been around for thousands of years, much longer than any government or country. The stories have historically proven to have powerful effects on the brain and body, forming intense connections between people and providing a path for human behaviors and morals.

But what makes for a good story? It is important for the story to affect different parts of the brain. If it is a good story, it might have funny parts, sad parts, and scary parts, all of which affect those different areas of the brain. From an evolutionary perspective, the parts of myth only work if both people engaged in the process have a brain for either creating or responding to the story. That is why stories that human beings tell one another are often catered to certain developmental stages. There are children's stories, adolescent stories, and adult stories. They are each tailored to the ways in which the brain functions at these different stages. For example, more complicated topics revealing the vagaries of life and love are reserved for adults. This same concept is true of stories in general, as human beings themselves evolved from earlier primates. As the human brain became more complex, there were more elaborate stories that were developed. We don't see fantastic stories, such as Greek myths, until after many thousands of years of *Homo sapien* evolution.

What is particularly interesting about connecting through myth is it also, at some levels, impacts how sexuality itself occurs. This has long been

---

30   Miller G. *The Mating Mind*. Anchor Books; 2001.

discussed in anthropological literature due to the number of indigenous cultures that do not incorporate the more Western tradition of monogamous marriage. In fact, there are several fairly unique groups in which the wedding night includes multiple men having sex with the bride, since it is believed that semen itself is what is sacred. In these instances, the entire society helps to raise each child, and the connection between a singular male and female is not as important.[31] These cultural beliefs are embodied in the myths of the various cultures, including the notion of multifatherhood, as well as providing for an overall sense of how the members of the group are to interact with each other when raising children.

When it comes to any mythic story about the connections that we make, it is important to recognize who or what exactly is included in that myth. If it is just a pair, then it is a very small nuclear family. The myth can also support the notion of a societal grouping, or even all of humanity. In that larger context, sexuality may ultimately be a representation of the overall connectedness of all human beings, or perhaps of human beings with God.

This latter point is particularly relevant in the context of religious myths. The majority of myths seem to have a basic structure in which two opposites are ultimately brought together in some unifying resolution. This takes advantage of a binary process in the brain that sets apart opposites. The brain is particularly good at creating opposites in our mind since this is exactly how the basics of the autonomic nervous system work. We need to know whether something is good or bad, or whether it is helpful or dangerous, and we then respond accordingly. When it comes to sexuality, we either get to mate or not mate. The brain works very well when it can narrow things down to one choice or another.

The fundamental oppositional concept present in religious myths is the relationship between human beings and God. The basic question is how a finite, fallible, and mortal being can have any kind of relationship with an infinite, perfect, and eternal being. It is through the mythic stories of God's interactions with various prophets, Messiahs, or even everyday people, that helps sort out what that relationship can look like. For example, in the Torah, we learn how to create a covenant with God by following

---

31   Margolis J. O: *The Intimate History of the Orgasm*. Grove Press; 2004.

various commandments such as worshiping a single God, following the sabbath, and getting a circumcision.

In the end, all of these myths can be embodied within rituals. And due to the complexities of the human brain, the rituals go far beyond mating rituals, incorporating many symbols, sensory stimuli, cognitive stimuli, and experiential elements. In a similar manner, this is exactly what unfolds during the mating rituals in human beings. As Geoffrey Miller points out, the dance between male and female can include art, poetry, music, and stories, all helping to generate the rhythms that are part of the ritual process bringing two individuals together.[32] More importantly, the rituals help to make myths more powerful by not having them only be part of a cognitive or emotional process, but also incorporating them as a physical process as well. When you pray or take part in a religious ceremony, it is not just about having some cognitive understanding about God; it is connecting your entire being with God—senses, emotions, thoughts, and experience.

ANCIENT MYTHS ABOUT SEX AND RELIGION

Perhaps one of the most interesting examples of an ancient myth linking sexuality and spirituality is a practice called sacred prostitution.[33] In sacred prostitution, women perform sexual acts for various, often random, men in or around the religious temple. Their engagement in sex was apparently part of the way to connect to a god or goddess. Thus, the term prostitution is slightly inaccurate in this case since the women were not performing the practice for money, but instead doing so as a spiritual duty. Some have argued that this behavior was beneficial for women as they were empowered through their actions and often held in high esteem by their communities.[34] However, others have expressed concern that this behavior contrib-

---

32   Miller G. *The Mating Mind*. Anchor Books; 2001.

33   Qualls-Corbett N. *The Sacred Prostitute: Eternal Aspect of the Feminine*. Inner City Books; 1988.

34   Budin SL. *The Myth of Sacred Prostitution in Antiquity*. Cambridge University Press; 2008.

uted to supporting patriarchal societies and ultimately was historically problematic for women. In either case, the myths regarding the meaning and importance of sacred prostitution demonstrate how various cultures and traditions engage sexuality as an integral component of spirituality.

The practice of sacred prostitution was deeply embedded in Mesopotamia in the Sumerian religion and mythology dating back to 4000 BCE. In Sumerian mythology, the goddess Inanna was associated with fertility, love, and war. As part of her religious cult, women would engage in sexual acts as a way of honoring the goddess and invoking her blessings.[35] The practice of sacred prostitution was not limited to the worship of Inanna, however. Other goddesses such as Nanshe and Ninlil were also associated with prostitution, and women would engage in sexual acts as part of their religious duties. Men could also participate in sacred prostitution, although this was less common than female prostitution.

In Hinduism, *devadasis* are women who are dedicated to serving a particular deity as part of their religious practice. Historically, devadasis were also involved in ritualized sex work, and their role in Hinduism has been a source of controversy and debate, particularly in recent times. The practice of dedicating women to temple service dates back as early as the fourth century BCE. Originally, devadasis were high-status women who were trained in music, dance, and other artistic pursuits as a means of serving the gods. However, over time, the role of devadasis became increasingly associated with sexual service to temple patrons—more aligned with what is historically regarded as prostitution.

The practice of temple prostitution was officially banned in India in the twentieth century, but the legacy of devadasis continues to impact modern Indian society. Many women who are descended from devadasi families continue to face discrimination and marginalization due to their perceived association with prostitution. Critics of the practice argue that it objectifies women and reinforces harmful gender stereotypes, while defenders of the practice argue that it is an important part of Hindu religious tradition.

The cult of Venus in Ephesus (in present day Turkey), a prominent city around 500 BCE also included sacred prostitutes who engaged in sexual

---

35   Leick G. *Sex and Eroticism in Mesopotamian Literature*. Routledge; 2010.

acts as part of their religious duties.[36] These women were known as *hiero-dules* and were seen as embodying the divine essence of Venus. In addition to sexual rites, the cult of Venus in Ephesus also involved the use of drugs, along with various rituals that included music and dance as a means of achieving a state of ecstasy and communion with the goddess.

While these ancient myths may seem alien to our modern-day way of thinking about spirituality, there are still pagan groups today that engage in sacred prostitution. The point here is that various myths have found ways of linking sexuality with religion, and then those myths are embodied in rituals.

Through the incorporation of the myths of these ancient traditions within rituals, they provide us with an opportunity to understand the meaning of the rituals as well as helping us to feel the meaning of the myths. As discussed in chapter 2, rituals can take on an entire continuum of experiences, ranging from basic feelings of connection with another in romance and love, a connection with an entire congregation or community, connection with all of humanity, or connection with the universe itself. The most powerful experiences during rituals are frequently referred to as "mystical." The myths help us to identify the basis of the experience through a discussion about enlightenment and spiritual transformation. Myths provide a source for talk about revelation and conversion. In short, the myths define the ecstasy that arises during sexual, as well as spiritual, experiences.

---

36   Dillon M. *Girls and Women in Classical Greek Religion*. Routledge; 2002.

CHAPTER 4

SEXUAL ECSTASY AND SPIRITUAL ECSTASY:

IMPACT ON THE BRAIN AND HUMAN HISTORY

I understood everything [about my experience], but cannot tell you what that means. I knew there was no death; tears rolled down my face, I sat there for, I don't know how long in a sea of total bliss, unspeakable joy, and felt a sense of peace that cannot be described—I had touched God.

—Subject from our Survey of Spiritual Experiences describing sexuality as part of their spiritual experience

The eye through which I see God is the same eye through which God sees me; my eye and God's eye are one eye, one seeing, one knowing, one love.

—Catholic sage and mystic Meister Eckhart

WHAT ARE SPIRITUAL EXPERIENCES?

What I find remarkable about the two quotes above is that mystical experiences have a powerful and transformative effect, whether you are a great mystic or an everyday person. This was one of the most important outcomes we found as a result of conducting our Survey of Spiritual Experiences. This was an online survey of the most intense spiritual experiences people had that we ran for about ten years, from 2007 until 2017. In it, we asked people about who they were, their religious and spiritual background, any circumstances around the experience, and then provided a textbox for respondents to write a narrative description of whatever they consider their most intense spiritual experience. The project produced a treasure trove of data, and we have already published a number of articles based on the accumulated data, including descriptions of the experiences and how the experiences affected people.[37]

Through a review of over 2000 survey participants' spiritual experiences, as well as those of famous mystics throughout history, we were able to derive the five experiential core elements. Our analysis revealed the presence of a sense of intensity, a sense of clarity, a sense of unity and connectedness, and a sense of surrender.[38] From the quote that begins this chapter, you can see that the person felt the intensity of "unspeakable joy," clarity in understanding everything, surrender in not knowing how long it was happening, and unity and connectedness by "touching" God. These characteristic elements make up the core components of mystical experiences. And they ultimately lead to a transformation of the person in body, mind, and spirit.

Importantly, each of these elements are associated with specific brain areas. The sense of intensity is associated with the emotional centers of the brain in the limbic structures. Brain scans conducted as a component of our studies have shown increased activity present in the amygdala and hippocampus during intense spiritual practices such as prayer or meditation.[39]

---

37   Yaden DB, Eichstaedt JC, Schwartz HA, et al. The language of ineffability: linguistic analysis of mystical experiences. *Psychology of Religion and Spirituality.* 8(3);244-252, 2016; Yaden DB, Haidt J, Hood RW, Vago DR, Newberg AB. The varieties of self-transcendent experience. *Review of General Psychology.* 2017;21(2):143-160.

38   Newberg AB, Waldman MR. *How Enlightenment Changes Your Brain: The New Science of Transformation.* Penguin Random House; 2016.

39   Newberg AB, Iversen J. The neural basis of the complex mental task of meditation: neurotransmitter and neurochemical considerations. *Med Hypotheses.* 2003;61(2):282-291; Monti DA, Kash KM, Kunkel EJ, et al. Changes in cerebral blood flow and anxiety associated with an 8-week mindfulness programme in women with breast cancer. *Stress Health.* 2012;28(5):397-407; Cohen DL, Wintering N, Tolles V, et al. Cerebral blood flow effects of yoga training: preliminary evaluation of 4 cases. *J Altern Complement Med.* 2009;15(1):9-14.

The sense of clarity is probably associated with a complex set of structures that might be centered on the thalamus. The thalamus is a central structure that connects many higher order brain regions and also brings sensory information into the brain, particularly from the ears and eyes. Throughout our studies, we have observed interesting shifts in the activity of the thalamus during spiritual practices. And we also have seen changes in the thalamus, even at rest, in long term practitioners who have been doing their practice for 20 years or more.[40]

In my prior work, we proposed that a sense of unity would be associated with a decrease of activity in the parietal lobe. In fact, we have now observed in many of our brain scan studies of spiritual practices—meditation, prayer, and a variety of others—that the parietal lobe appears to quiet down when people experience a loss of the sense of self and an increased sense of connection with other people, the universe, or God.[41] This makes sense since the parietal lobe is particularly important in taking sensory information and creating our sense of self. If increased activity in the parietal lobe helps to generate our sense of self, then a decrease should be associated with a loss of that sense of self. Further, the parietal lobe is involved in helping us to distinguish between objects in the world around us. A decrease in this area of the brain should be associated with the inability to perceive discrete objects leading to a sense of oneness or interconnectedness of all things. The importance of the parietal lobe has also been observed in patients with various brain lesions. One study showed that patients who had abnormalities in their parietal lobe were more likely to express feelings of self-transcendence (or getting beyond the self) than those who had lesions in other parts of the brain.[42]

---

40   Newberg AB, Wintering N, Waldman MR, Amen D, Khalsa DS, Alavi A. Cerebral blood flow differences between long-term meditators and non-meditators. *Conscious Cogn.* 2010;19(4):899-905.

41   Newberg A, d'Aquili E, Rause V. *Why God Won't Go Away: Brain Science and the Biology of Belief.* Ballantine Books; 2001; Newberg AB, Iversen J. The neural basis of the complex mental task of meditation: neurotransmitter and neurochemical considerations. *Med Hypotheses.* 2003;61(2):282-291.

42   Urgesi C, Aglioti SM, Skrap M, Fabbro F. The spiritual brain: selective cortical lesions modulate human self-transcendence. *Neuron.* 2010;65(3):309-319. doi:10.1016/j.neuron.2010.01.026.

The sense of surrender during these experiences is most likely associated with decreased activity in the frontal lobes. When the frontal lobes turn on, you are likely to experience a sense of alertness and focused attention. This frequently occurs in the early phases of spiritual practices such as meditation and prayer. When you focus on an object of meditation or prayer, you use your frontal lobes. Essentially, the frontal lobes are in charge of willful behavior and actions. But if the frontal lobes experience a drop in activity, you may feel as if you are no longer in charge of what's going on. You may lose your sense of focus and feel as if you have surrendered or let go of your will. At this point, you are essentially along for the ride, and that is exactly what is described during mystical experiences.

Finally, the autonomic nervous system is highly involved in these experiences. We previously proposed that mystical experiences are characterized by the most intense physiological processes that include the mutually intense activation of the sympathetic and parasympathetic nervous systems. This is the fifth possible interaction between the two arms of the autonomic nervous system that we discussed in chapter 2. This mutual activation is associated with powerful feelings of arousal and ecstasy along with profound bliss, but to a stronger degree than any other experience. These are the mystical, or enlightenment, experiences that have been described since the earliest traditions were passed down. But remember that the mutual activity of the autonomic nervous system is likely built into our brain and body because of sex. Both systems turn on during sexual orgasm, thus leading to sexual ecstasy—the powerful force behind our drive to procreate. In this way, sexual and spiritual ecstasy are deeply linked in our biology.

While we can find that individual brain areas are involved with the core aspects of spiritual experiences, these brain areas all work together as part of a complex interconnected network. In fact, much of the recent cognitive neuroscience research has focused on brain networks such as the *salience network* that tells us what is important, or the *default mode network* that is on when our brain is at rest. Ultimately, the brain is a massive, interconnected network that enables our experiences, emotions, and cognitions to become interwoven in our experience of our self and our reality.

THE TRANSFORMATIONAL BRAIN

The final characteristic of intense, mystical experiences is their transformational effect on the individual. What this means is that everyone who has had such an experience appears to be completely changed by it. These are experiences of enlightenment and transformation. In our Survey of Spiritual Experiences, people reported substantial changes in how they approached their interpersonal relationships, their jobs, their sense of meaning and purpose in life, their sense of religion and spirituality, and even how they viewed life and death as a result of their experience.

What is amazing about such transformations is that they appear to occur in a matter of minutes, or even seconds. This is not typically how we think of the brain working. We learn things over many months, or even years, as we develop our brain processes for mathematics or language. But for some reason, these intense experiences seem to change the person's entire way of being in moments. Frankly, we don't know how this happens. We don't know if these experiences unlock pathways that had previously been inactive, or if perhaps the entire brain is rewired. Either way, these ecstatic experiences change people forever. This is born out in our survey, as well as other similar data from other researchers, which shows that the effects can last a lifetime.[43]

CONNECTING THE MYSTICAL WITH THE SEXUAL

We have already considered in chapter 2 how the arousal and quiescent parts of the brain and body can lead to similar experiences between spirituality and sexuality. In both circumstances, the arousal and quiescent parts turn on in a complex rhythm that can induce powerful experiences. The changes in the autonomic nervous system are connected to the hypothalamus. As you get into the physical rhythms of sex itself, you drive the hypothalamus activity. But the hypothalamus is connected through the

---

43 Newberg AB, Waldman MR. *How Enlightenment Changes Your Brain: The New Science of Transformation*. Penguin Random House; 2016.

thalamus to the amygdala which becomes activated by all of this important rhythmic activity. As the amygdala turns on, its connections to the higher cortical areas such as the frontal and parietal lobe lead to these areas shutting down.

What would such an effect look like? When the amygdala turns on during sex, it is associated with a strong sense of emotional intensity—just like what happens in mystical experiences. When the thalamus shifts its activity, a powerful sense of clarity arises—just like what happens in mystical experiences. When the parietal lobe shuts down, we have seen that there is a loss of the sense of self and a sense of oneness—just like what happens in mystical experiences. When the frontal lobe shuts down, we have seen that there is a sense of willful surrender or letting go—just like what happens in mystical experiences.

In our Survey of Spiritual Experiences, one man described the intersection of spirituality and sex during a particularly dramatic *Kundalini* awakening. Kundalini refers to a vital energy, typically feminine in origin, that runs through the body and when cultivated and awakened, can lead to enlightenment:

Seven years ago, while in meditation, a strange feeling overcame me. The room I was in began to take on a silvery-blue glow, and I sensed a presence. Everything looked freshly washed, cleaned, and shimmering. The feeling of a presence grew stronger, and I had the feeling something was going to happen.

All of a sudden, I got an erection. This was no ordinary erection. My penis felt like it was the size of a telephone pole, and it was just as hard. So hard it was painful. There was an extremely strong sexual feeling in the head of my penis, which proceeded to travel DOWN the shaft to the perineum muscle. The presence I was experiencing was extremely strong. What had started out as sexual feelings seemed to be compressing into a shaft of light energy. I could feel it "humming." I tried to relax into what was taking place. I felt as though I was a bystander watching something take control of my body.

As soon as I just thought to relax, I felt a tearing at the base of my spine, a sharp pain that lasted only a few seconds, and this energy was now in my spine. I can only describe the sensation being that of a huge penis inside a vagina. I could actually feel "my" penis in "my" vagina, even though I have no idea what it feels like to have a vagina!

There seemed to be a slight haze in front of my eyes, which was visible no matter what direction I looked in. My breathing went from deep and erratic to somewhat shallow. I then realized that I was no longer breathing in the normal fashion, but was now breathing through my spinal column. With each inhale I felt the energy being sucked up my spinal column. The sexual aspect of it was full blown.

Looking at my hands I could "see" the vibration. Everything was clear as a bell, no matter what I looked at. I could see detail that normally would be impossible to see. It then dawned on me that although I was physically in a state of quivering sexuality, my mental capacities were sharpening. My awareness was expanding.

I didn't have long to ponder what was going on because the next thing I knew my body was moving. It was as if someone had physically altered the way my body was positioned. I felt my hips pushed back, my pelvis thrust forward, and my entire spinal column snapped into a different position. There was no pain with this sudden movement, and it seemed to open the way for this energy to come up the back of the neck, at which point it felt like my penis was in my mouth. My entire being was expanding, and I realized that it (my being) was intelligent and had a mind of its own. I was a witness to an intelligence within me that was far superior to my own. I instinctively knew that it meant me no harm; it was bringing me to orgasm.

The bluish-white energy began to "suck" the golden energy up my spine and I felt my entire being drawn into my head. At the moment of orgasm, I became whole and complete, one with the all. I was male and female, I was neither. I was as big as existence itself, and as small as the smallest atom. There was no good or evil, right or wrong, this or that. Only "being."

Combining this new data from the Survey of Spiritual Experiences, along with the findings from our brain imaging studies, we can clearly see the spiritual brain ties directly to the sexual brain. This information may also be important for so many people who have had intense spiritual experiences only to find them linked to sexual feelings, but have not been able to understand why that would happen. In fact, this data can take the stigma out of sexuality in the context of religious and spiritual experience. We can now show that it is spiritually and biologically reasonable to connect sexuality and sexual energy with powerful experiences.

Thus, not only are the neurobiological processes of sexuality and spirituality the same, but they also appear to be connected through the evolution of the human brain through mating. This system evolved so that mating could occur as effectively as possible. It turns out that spirituality can help us access this system almost, if not more than, effectively as sex. This relationship is extremely important in not only connecting sexual and spiritual ecstasy but in revealing how this connection leads to so many other aspects of religion and spirituality.

SPIRITUAL EXPERIENCE AND HUMAN CIVILIZATION

There is one other interesting point about the powerful link between sexuality and spirituality, and that has to do with how spiritual experiences influence human history. It is currently believed that religion clearly preceded the development of civilization. The earliest evidence of spiritual beliefs comes from the burials of Neanderthals over 100,000 years ago; civilizations formed only 5,000 years ago. The recent archaeological find of the temple at Gobekli Tepe, Turkey, dates back 10,000 years. This temple's ritualistic animal carvings clearly indicate that organized religious activities preceded the establishment of city states.

It's fascinating that there appears to be no evidence of any civilization developing without some type of highly complex religious activities.

Ancient Egyptians, Mesopotamians, Aztecs, Mayans, and the people of Easter Island all based their society on religion and spirituality; their cosmologies and mythologies reflect moral codes that were congruent in both the worlds of spirit and flesh. It is important to note that all complex societies are loaded with rituals that extend beyond religion. There are rituals for work, play, education, and politics—all springing from mating rituals.

The latter aspect of humanity—politics—seems to have a particularly intriguing origin when it comes to sex and the brain. Forgetting all of the sexual escapades of kings, queens, and presidents throughout history, the point I want to make is how we end up with these leaders in the first place. Not the specific ones that we have, but why we seem to revere or worship leaders.

Where does the concept of worship come from? You guessed it—sex, and its expression in the complexity of the mating process. In any hierarchical group of animals, there is almost always a leader of some kind. Think of the queen bee or the alpha male in a wolf pack. The entire group reveres these high-ranking animals in order to create group stability. If the alpha male is continually fighting off other males, the group will be on shaky grounds. Alphas must be able to create a sense of stability over time that enables the entire group to function properly in order to survive. To do this, they must be strong, but the other members of the group must defer to them for the most part.

It's the same in human society. Frequently deposing presidents or monarchs is destabilizing. Rules and rituals support the stability of the leaders and help ensure that the rest of society continues to recognize the importance of those leaders. In Britain and France, when a monarch dies, they immediately say: "The King is dead. Long live the King (or Queen)!" This seemingly contradictory phrase simultaneously announces the death of the previous monarch and assures the people that there will be stability and continuity by saluting the new monarch. These ideas are the descendants of the biological imperative for sexual stability within animal groups. Not to belabor the point, but this is yet another lens through which to look at the manner in which emotional and cognitive brain areas enable human beings to create complex social mores and structured societies. These brain areas owe their origins to the basic processes related to sexuality and mating, and, subsequently, they evolve into religious and spiritual concepts and then into civilizations.

A recent detailed description of the evolutionary forces that may have operated to enhance religious activity in human beings is presented in the book, *The Emergence and Evolution of Religion*.[44] The authors indicate that religion evolved due to Darwinian and Spencerian selection since religion was individually adaptive, but also was beneficial for social and geopolitical purposes for establishing close-knit groups. The research presented herein provides an underlying neurobiological basis for such an argument showing how sexuality and spirituality are connected, and how those biological forces led to the broader social influences of religion on the brain.

UNVEILING THE ROOTS OF MATRIARCHAL AND PATRIARCHAL SOCIETIES

When it comes to the structure of civilizations, it seems that a fundamental aspect is whether they tend toward a patriarchal (male dominated) or matriarchal (female dominated) system. The emergence and perpetuation of matriarchal and/or patriarchal societies has been the subject of profound scholarly exploration, with various theories attempting to elucidate the roots of these social structures. Interestingly, in both cases, not only does leadership stem more from males or females, but such systems justify their approach through mythic elements that literally begin with either a male or female origin to the universe. For example, in monotheistic traditions, God is regarded as the "Father," while in many indigenous cultures, "Mother Earth" is the foundation of our existence. Early scholarship in this area was written by the Swiss anthropologist and jurist named Johann Bachofen who argued that motherhood was the source of human society, religion, and morality.[45] Importantly, there was a transition through time from the matriarchal perspective that existed in early human history that was eradicated by the patriarchal perspective that appears to exist through most cultures today.

---

44   Turner JH, Maryanski A, Petersen AK, Geertz AW. *The Emergence of and Evolution of Religion*. Routledge; 2018.

45   Bachofen JJ. Manheim R. (Translator). *Myth, Religion, and Mother Right. Princeton University Press, 1992.*

Although controversial, his ideas are somewhat consistent with what we have come to understand about the human brain, sexuality, and spirituality.

The mythic concepts of a male- or female-dominated spiritual, cosmological, and ontological model ultimately support the entire political structure of the society. Based on the information we have considered in this book, much of whether a matriarchal or patriarchal system develops has to do with mating rituals and how those rituals affect the brain. Of course, there are many factors including economic dynamics, religious influences, and power structures that contribute to the establishment and maintenance of patriarchal or matriarchal norms.

If we begin with "ladies first," one theory posits that matriarchal societies emerge from matrilineal kinship systems, where descent and inheritance are traced through the female line.[46] For example, according to the halakha, which is the collective body of Jewish religious law, you are considered Jewish if your mother is, not based on what your father is. Such a framework challenges the traditional patrilineal structures and emphasizes the pivotal role of women in familial and societal organization.

As mentioned above, there is likely a strong connection between matriarchal societies and the worship of female deities or the veneration of the divine feminine. This spiritual foundation is believed to have elevated the status of women, fostering a societal structure where their influence extended beyond familial roles.

Anthropological studies propose that matriarchal societies may have originated in egalitarian hunter-gatherer communities. In such societies, the absence of a rigid hierarchy allowed for more equitable distribution of resources and decision-making, providing women with opportunities to assume leadership roles.[47]

Economic theories argue that matriarchal structures may arise in societies where women have economic autonomy. In situations where women

---

46   Goettner-Abendroth, H. Societies of Peace: Matriarchies Past, Present and Future. In E.
      N. Gladden & S. Strozier (Eds.), *Feminist Theory and the Study of Folklore* (pp. 15-30).
      University of Illinois Press.

47   Gimbutas M. *The Civilization of the Goddess: The World of Old Europe*. HarperOne;
      1991. Eisler R. *The Chalice and the Blade: Our History, our Future*. HarperOne; 1987.

contribute significantly to the economic well-being of the community, their influence and decision-making authority are likely to be more pronounced.[48]

Another perspective suggests that matriarchal societies develop as a response to various external challenges, emphasizing social stability and cooperation. In situations where collaboration and consensus-building are valued, women may play central roles in decision-making processes, contributing to the emergence of matriarchal structures.[49] Along these lines, environmental determinism proposes that the physical and geographical characteristics of a region can shape social structures. Matriarchal societies may emerge in environments where resources are abundant and the need for hierarchical control is less pressing, allowing for more egalitarian social structures.[50]

Patriarchal systems develop for related but distinct reasons. One prevalent theory posits that the shift toward patriarchal societies occurred alongside the advent of agriculture primarily because this established ownership of land.[51] Once you have property ownership, it becomes important to know how that land is transferred from one person to another. Buying and selling, or perhaps bartering in ancient times, is one way, but what about how land is managed within family ownership? One way to do this is by passing down ownership within patrilineal lines. This shift led to the consolidation of power in male hands, establishing a patriarchal framework.[52] Males wanted to control females in a manner that made mating more likely to occur. However, it must also be realized that this focus on resources by males is partially driven by the sexual selection of

48 Sanday PR. *Women at the Center: Life in a Modern Matriarchy*. Cornell University Press; 2004.

49 Bamberger J, Tuzin D. Women in the language and society of the Kung. *Int J Women's Studies*. 1975; 3(1): 5-27.

50 Boserup E. *Women's Role in Economic Development*. St. Martin's Press; 1970.

51 Lerner G. *The Creation of Patriarchy*. Oxford University Press; 1986.

52 Yoffee N. *Myths of the Archaic State: Evolution of the Earliest Cities, States, and Civilizations*. Cambridge University Press; 2005.

females for mates with more resources.[53] Thus, "We come from a long and unbroken line of ancestral fathers who succeeded in obtaining mates, preventing their infidelity, and providing enough benefits to keep them from leaving. We also come from a long line of ancestral mothers who granted sexual access to men who provided beneficial resources."[54]

Along these same lines, economic theories propose that patriarchal structures are closely tied to control over resources. As societies transitioned from nomadic or communal living to settled agricultural practices, the accumulation of property and wealth became significant. Men, being traditionally associated with physical strength, assumed dominant roles in managing and safeguarding these resources.[55] If they are going to fight and potentially die defending their land, then they get to own that land. And if they conquer someone else's land, then the conquering males get to take control of that land as well.

As such power expanded, social and political power dynamics contributed significantly to the formation of patriarchal societies. The concept of hegemony, as developed by Antonio Gramsci,[56] suggests that dominant groups maintain control not only through force but also by shaping cultural norms and values. Patriarchy is thus perpetuated through the normalization of male dominance in various spheres.

Subsequently, the impact of colonialism is another lens through which patriarchy is understood. Colonial powers often imposed their patriarchal structures on indigenous societies, influencing social hierarchies and gender relations. Postcolonial societies may grapple with the legacies of these structures.[57]

Finally, like matriarchal societies, many patriarchal systems have roots in religious and mythical narratives that reinforce male dominance. The association of divine authority with male deities, coupled with creation

---

53   Buss DM. *Evolution of Desire: Strategies of Human Mating.* Basic Books; 2016.

54   Buss DM. *Evolution of Desire: Strategies of Human Mating.* Basic Books; 2016.

55   Boserup E. *Women's Role in Economic Development.* St. Martin's Press; 1970.

56   Gramsci A. *Selections from the Prison Notebooks.* International Publishers; 1971.

57   Mohanty CT. Under Western Eyes: Feminist Scholarship and Colonial Discourses. *Feminist Review.* 1988;30, 61-88.

myths that prioritize male roles, has played a crucial role in legitimizing patriarchal structures.[58]

Despite the richness of these theories, it is essential to acknowledge the challenges and criticisms they face. The scarcity of direct archaeological evidence and the influence of cultural biases pose hurdles in accurately reconstructing the histories of matriarchal and patriarchal societies. The diverse and multifaceted nature of societies makes it challenging to pinpoint a singular cause or origin of matriarchal or patriarchal systems. Moreover, the term "matriarchy" itself is often debated, as some argue that true matriarchies, with women holding uncontested power, are rare or nonexistent.[59] There are important implications for considering how various systems that are based on a matriarchy or patriarch come about. By unraveling the theories surrounding patriarchal societies, scholars contribute to ongoing discussions about gender equity, social justice, and the potential for transformative change in societies around the world.

THE BIOLOGICAL BASIS OF MATRIARCHAL AND PATRIARCHAL SYSTEMS

In this book, we have continually returned to the human brain as a fundamental source for our beliefs and behaviors. While this has focused on religions, we also must acknowledge the overlap with social systems of governance. As we have done all along, it is important to recognize the similarities between the spiritual and sexual, and in this case, the political. In fact, it is interesting to consider how religions regard males and females in terms of their own leadership roles. In Catholicism, only males can be priests and every pope has been a male. In the orthodox Jewish and Muslim traditions, only males can be rabbis or imams. Religions such as Buddhism and Hinduism typically do not have the same kind of leadership hierarchy

58   Oyěwùmí O. *The Invention of Women: Making an African Sense of Western Gender Discourses.* University of Minnesota Press; 1997.

59   Sanday PR. *Women at the Center: Life in a Modern Matriarchy.* Cornell University Press; 2004.

as the monotheistic traditions, however, they too tend to be male dominated. When you consider almost every society from ancient Mesopotamia
to Europe, Asia, Africa, and the indigenous tribes throughout the world,
only about 10–20% of leaders have been women. This raises the important
question—Why?

As we have considered above, there are many theories that lead to
matriarchal or patriarchal societies. But how does the biology of sex and
mating come into play? As with all theories, it is difficult to be definitive.
Biological essentialism theories argue that the physical differences between
men and women, particularly related to reproductive roles, have been used
to justify gendered divisions of labor. This has perpetuated the notion of
men as providers and women as caregivers, reinforcing patriarchal norms.[60]

THE DANCE OF POWER: MATING STRATEGIES AND THE DEVELOPMENT OF MALE AND FEMALE DOMINATED SOCIETIES

The dynamics of power within societies have long been shaped by various
factors, including mating strategies. Mating strategies encompass the behaviors and tactics individuals employ to attract and secure mates, and
these strategies play a pivotal role in the development of both male and
female-dominated societies.

In some species, females exhibit a preference for mates with access
to valuable resources.[61] This preference can lead to the development of
male-dominated societies where males compete to accumulate resources as
a means of attracting mates. This dynamic is observed in various animal
species and has parallels in human societies where resource acquisition is
linked to social status. We mentioned this above, but what is important
is how this is actually related to sexual selection. Men with more power

---

60   Connell RW. *Gender and Power: Society, the Person, and Sexual Politics*. Stanford Uni-
      versity Press; 1987.

61   Buss DM. Sex differences in human mate preferences: Evolutionary hypotheses tested in
      37 cultures. *Behavior Brain Sci*. 1989;12(1): 1-49.

and resources were part of what attracted sexual partners. After all, women would reason that a male with substantial resources, particularly food and shelter, would provide a better environment for her to raise her child successfully. And if this were the case, then future generations would seek similar characteristics in mates. Thus, an entire society would slowly evolve focused on the maintenance of male resources.

Female mate choice is not the sole determinant of mating dynamics. In certain species, females engage in intrasexual competition, competing with each other for access to high-quality mates.[62] This competition can contribute to the development of female-dominated societies where social hierarchies are shaped by female-female interactions.

Mating strategies and societal structures are not static; they evolve over time. Changes in cultural norms, economic systems, and access to education can alter mating dynamics and, consequently, power structures. Understanding historical shifts in mating strategies provides insights into the emergence and decline of male or female-dominated societies.

The relationship between mating strategies and the development of male or female-dominated societies is a complex interplay of evolutionary, cultural, and psychological factors. While evolutionary processes shape fundamental aspects of mating behavior, cultural influences and societal structures also play critical roles. Exploring these dynamics provides a deeper understanding of the intricate dance between biology and culture that underlies the power dynamics within human societies.

In the end, it seems clear that the development of civilizations and their power structures, particularly as they relate to religious and spiritual beliefs, is based on how our brain evaluates and responds to those structures. The brain's ability to worship leaders, understand social hierarchy, and establish connections with others is crucial. But these elements of human civilization are ultimately based on the neurophysiology of the mating process. Thus, sexuality and mating are what lead to the interweaving of religious and spiritual myths that support the social and political structure of the civilization.

---

62   Geary DC, Vigil J, & Byrd-Craven J. Evolution of human mate choice. *J Sex Res.* 2004;41(1), 27-42; Eagly AH, Wood, W. The origins of sex differences in human behavior: Evolved dispositions versus social roles. *Amer Psychologist.* 1999;54(6), 408-423.

PART II

THE CONNECTION BETWEEN SEX, SPIRITUALITY, AND SCIENCE

CHAPTER 5

ORGASMIC MEDITATION:

MAKING THE CONNECTION

I feel God, as well as a new and complete connection to people, myself, and life. I feel no separation or boundaries of my body. I feel expansiveness, ecstasy, and universal compassion. I feel life particles as though the universe is inside my own body. I hear God talk to me, and I talk to God.

—Study participant describing their experience during OM

FINDING THE DATA

Now that we have considered how spirituality and sexuality are linked through biology, the question is whether this is just some far flung idea or whether there is more definitive data that can support this contention. But to get this data, we would need some kind of practice that more directly links sexuality and spirituality. We would need an approach that actually uses sexuality to connect us to something spiritual. But what would that look like? We know that there are ancient approaches, such as Tantric yoga, that use sex to achieve spiritual experiences. But as is often the case with my research, we can only study people we know about and can find, and I was not familiar with any groups that did Tantric yoga who might be able to participate in a research study.

I had long pondered how to connect sexuality and spirituality, since this would provide a fundamental link between the animal rituals that are mating rituals and human rituals that are not only mating rituals but become expanded into every part of life, particularly religion and spirituality.

Although Gene d'Aquili and I discussed the possibility of designing a research study to clarify the relationship between sexuality and spirituality over 30 years ago, it had to wait until a phone call out of nowhere.

I was sitting in my office one early spring afternoon, reviewing several new research brain scans on my computer, when my phone rang. This in itself was unusual since my phone is in a back office, so I didn't really know how anyone would find that number. But sometimes people call our front desk and get transferred through, so I thought maybe it was important, or hopefully just an accident. I picked up the phone and a young woman's voice on the other end introduced herself and told me that she was a practitioner of orgasmic meditation, or OM, and she asked me if I knew anything about it. I told her that I did not, so she proceeded to explain that the practice involves the manual stimulation of a woman's clitoris. But she was insistent that this did not result in sexual stimulation so much as it formed a focus of the mind and consciousness for spiritual purposes. She had heard of my work studying spiritual practices and asked me if I would have any interest in studying this one.

My first thought was, "That sounds a little weird." But in my years of researching spiritual practices and experiences, I had gotten pretty used to things that were weird. In fact, I have often thought that the phrase "that seems weird" may be one of the most important statements leading to big scientific discoveries, so I was also intrigued. As I reflected on how she was describing this unique practice that combined sexual stimulation and meditation, I thought to myself, "Could this be the practice that combines sexuality and spirituality that I have been hoping to study for the past 30 years? Could this provide invaluable data helping us understand the link between sexuality and spirituality?" I certainly had to find out more.

She went on to describe the practice in great detail to me as I knew that this information would be critical for designing any kind of study looking at this particular practice. First of all, it was very specifically timed to last exactly 15 minutes. From a research perspective, this timing was actually quite important and helpful. When we study spiritual practices, many are open-ended in terms of their timing. With these open-ended practices, it is very challenging to know exactly when to initiate a brain scan to capture the peak moments of a person's spiritual practice or experience. In our earliest studies of meditation and prayer, many of the practices were done internally, in complete silence, with little observable body movements. We had no real way of knowing what a research subject was doing inside their mind or when they were doing it. We had to ask them to provide some kind of "signal," such as tugging on a string, to let us know when they were heading toward their peak moments. But a primary concern was always the temporary interruption that even tugging on a string might cause. How much would such a maneuver disturb a person's deep meditative state? But having a practice that is well-timed makes it clear as to when to do a scan of the brain.

She went on to explain the different elements of the practice. She stated that it requires two people. This is also an intriguing element of OM as it is one of the few practices that is done by a pair of individuals working together. Initially, they spend a few minutes doing something called "grounding" in which they effectively welcome each other and confirm that they are about to perform the practice. This preliminary stage is similar to many other types of ritual practices that might involve preparing sacred objects on a table, lighting candles, or burning incense. And in many religious traditions, there are even practices or prayers that introduce the larger spiritual program. For example, in Judaism, the *Bar'chu* prayer is said early in a service as a way of calling people to prayer—praising God and exclaiming that the prayers about to be said as part of the service are directed toward God. Thus, this concept of grounding is rooted in the practices of many religious and spiritual traditions.

Another interesting aspect of the OM practice is how they prepare a space for the practice. This "nest" is created through the use of pillows and blankets to create a comfortable space to perform the practice. In thinking through a research study, I realized that it would be relatively easy to create such a space in one of the rooms in our lab so that they could feel as comfortable as possible performing the practice. This has long been a challenge for us in our research studies since most spiritual practices are performed in spiritual places. We have questioned whether a nun performing prayer outside of a church, or a Muslim praying outside of a mosque, can generate the same kind of experience. Much has been written about "sacred architecture" as these spaces are embedded with meaning (e.g., churches built in the shape of a cross), have portrayals of religious concepts (e.g., images of a prophet or religious stories on the walls or windows), and typically have impressive stature (e.g., high ceilings and echoing silence). All of these characteristics help make sacred spaces sacred and provide an environment that brings about intense spiritual feelings.

Location, location, location is essential in real estate, but it turns out that it is very important in religion and spirituality as well. We have always tried to create a space conducive to spiritual practices and experiences within a laboratory setting—not always an easy thing to do. However, the OM practice might make that issue a little easier since they can actually bring their sacred space into the lab itself.

Once the nest is set up, the person who strokes the clitoris (the stroker, or what we sometimes referred to as the "giver"), sits on the floor beside the person being stimulated (the strokee or what we sometimes called the "receiver"). In our lab, we used "giver" and "receiver" because we had studied some other practices in which there was a directionality with some people being givers and other people being receivers. So, these terms also provided a context for our research team.

Perhaps the greatest challenge in studying OM is the way people are positioned and move during the practice. Previous fMRI studies of sexual orgasm were performed with people in the scanner while they self-stimulated their genitals. By masturbating to the point of climax, they could evaluate the changes in the brain associated with sexual stimulation and orgasm. However, while some movement likely occurred, since it was self-stimulation, it could be performed in a scanner. But with OM, both people are seated beside one another, and one person needs to be able to touch the other's clitoris. Thus, we quickly realized that there would be no way to actually have people conduct the practice in the scanner itself. Of course, we could scan them before and after the practice, which we did, but we really wanted to capture the peak moment of OM.

For this, we turned to a nuclear medicine imaging technique called positron emission tomography (PET) imaging. We had used it and a similar one called SPECT imaging (single photon emission computed tomography) to study many other spiritual practices that involved movement or positions that were not amenable to being in a scanner.

PET imaging begins by placing a small intravenous catheter into a vein of a person's arm. This provides a portal for injection of a small amount of a radioactive tracer that follows some part of the body's or brain's physiology. In the case of PET imaging, the most commonly used tracer is Fluorodeoxyglucose (FDG), which is basically a radioactive sugar, with the fluorine atom being the radioactive part that is detected by the scanner, and the deoxyglucose being the sugar. Since the brain uses sugar for energy, it takes up this radioactive sugar when it is functioning. The brain works in a nice way such that the more a particular part of the brain is working, the more sugar it takes up. And if a part of the brain quiets down, it takes up less sugar. So, by injecting the radioactive sugar, we can see patterns of activity that are associated with different mental states.

The important thing about this tracer is that after it circulates for a few minutes, it gets into the brain and undergoes a metabolic change that effectively traps it within the nerve cells. This allows us to capture a "snapshot" of the brain at a time that corresponds with the minutes shortly after injection. For example, if I were to inject you while you were reading this book and then have you finish reading, check your mail, get into your car, drive over to your closest imaging facility, and undergo a scan, the scan could tell me what your brain was doing while you were reading this book. The other activities wouldn't affect the scan results. We have used this technique to study many different types of practices, particularly those that involve movement or specific body positions that are not conducive to being in a scanner itself.

It was eventually decided that PET imaging would be our best option to be able to study the OM practice directly. We noted that we could set the study up in such a way to inject both the stroker and strokee at the same time. We could then put both of them in the scanner after the practice and it would tell us what was happening at the moment of the practice. Because of the 15-minute practice time limit and the FDG degradation rate, we decided it was best to inject people halfway through the practice so that the minutes following the injection would correspond to the last, and most intense, part of the OM practice.

At the very end of the practice, the two individuals participate in a closing component called "sharing frames." Much like many other spiritual practices, this closing element is an important way of bringing the entire practice to a conclusion. This tells the participant's brains they are returning to everyday life activities and they are no longer engaged in the spiritual practice.

After it was explained to me how the OM practice worked, I became more excited about the possibility of studying it. Because of its clearly defined elements, it seemed an ideal practice to study from a scientific perspective.

The phone call continued and I went on to explain my background in studying spiritual phenomena over the past 30 years. I mentioned that one of the missing components was trying to bridge the intersection between sexuality and spirituality. I described to her our early research exploring how rituals in animals eventually evolved into rituals in humans. These all started out as mating rituals, the basis for sexuality. Of course, rituals in humans became vastly expanded into so many other areas of life, particularly religious and spiritual activities.

She was very excited to hear this because one of the principal concerns about the OM practice is whether it just represents sexual stimulation, or perhaps something more. Certainly, the practitioners feel that there is something more to OM, but they worry that others might not see it that way.

One way I tried probing to see if I could better differentiate the sexual and spiritual parts of OM was by asking her what kinds of experiences the OM practitioners typically had. She proceeded to describe feelings of oneness and connectedness both with the other person in the paired practice as well as broader experiences of oneness with the universe. She also described that people felt a sense of release or letting go. And finally, she explained how the practice is frequently associated with very intense emotional responses, as well as a feeling of powerful energy rising up through the body. She did not however describe feelings of arousal, desire, or love that typically occur during sex.

Her descriptions of OM resonated with me deeply because of my prior work on the study of intense spiritual, or enlightenment, experiences. In fact, in our Survey of Spiritual Experiences, the core elements included a sense of oneness or unity, a sense of intensity, and a sense of letting go. That the core elements of intense spiritual experiences seem to be elicited by this rather brief type of spiritual practice that involves sexual stimulation was fascinating to me and clearly demonstrated that this was an interesting hybrid practice—just the kind I was looking for.

That such experiences can be reliably reproduced in relatively brief periods of time during OM speaks to the close relationship between sexuality and spirituality. If we could document this both phenomenologically as well as neurophysiologically, we might really have found the link between sexuality and mating rituals with spirituality and religious rituals. Of course, this all sounds good on paper, but the devil is in the details as they always say. So, we embarked on development of a study to look at 20 couples performing the OM practice in our lab while using PET scans to assess the neurophysiological effects. I should note that we have a unique scanner that performs both PET and MRI at the same time, so not only were we able to see how OM affected metabolism in the brain, but we could also look at persisting effects based on the functional MRI data we also acquired after the practice was done. We will discuss the MRI information later in the chapter, but it provided another layer of understanding how the OM practice works.

THE RESULTS ARE IN!

After about a year of bringing people into our lab to perform the OM practice in the midst of the COVID pandemic, I finally had the opportunity to sit down with the data and see what changes occurred.

The results did not disappoint.

First, and perhaps most important, we asked people whether they felt that the OM session was comparable to their typical OM sessions in more natural environments. Overall, the group rated them a 9.7 out of 10 in terms of comparability. And they rated the experiences a 6.6 out of 10 in terms of intensity. Thus, we felt pretty good that we were able to re-create the OM practice in our lab. This is always an essential aspect of studying spiritual practices as I mentioned before. If we want to study a prayer practice but the person is unable to do it, then the results are meaningless. It is crucial to know whether or not the person is actually able to enter into a spiritual state in a manner similar to their usual experiences. This certainly seemed to be the case with the OM people in our study.

But what happened in their brains?

When we looked at the PET scan findings, we started by looking at the entire group, and then broke it down into the males (the strokers or givers) and females (the strokees or receivers). We thought that these different analyses would be important to understand how the OM practice works in general and how it works differently for the givers and the receivers.

When we looked at the entire group, we found several important and significant changes that occurred during the OM practice. We saw decreases in frontal lobe activity, as well as decreases in parietal lobe activity. These changes are important because, if you remember, such decreases more resemble a meditative practice rather than sexual stimulation. In fact, studies of sexual stimulation typically demonstrate a brain becoming more and more active. But during OM, the brain seems to start quieting down in most areas.

The decrease in frontal lobe activity is probably associated with a sense of letting go or release. The frontal lobes are involved in helping us focus attention on whatever tasks we have at hand. Studies of meditation and prayer that involve intense focus on various objects or phrases typically result in increased frontal lobe activity. However, practices involving a sense of release or letting go have been associated with decreased frontal lobe activity. Interestingly, decreased frontal lobe activity has also been reported in flow states as well as in highly creative states such as jazz improvisation. These are all states in which a person feels as if their own consciousness is no longer in control of the process, and the process is simply happening to them. They are along for the ride. That this occurs during OM makes sense in terms of the kind of experience practitioners report as provided by one of the females in our study:

> I felt as if I was following him, as if he was leading me into and through the meditation. I felt surrendered. I felt out of control, and I felt safe. It was exhilarating and scary at the same time.

Another area associated with the frontal lobes was also affected: the anterior cingulate gyrus. The anterior cingulate sits between the frontal lobe and the emotional areas of the brain's limbic system, and it functions as a kind of fulcrum between our frontal lobe concentration and executive processes and our emotions. It helps regulate the balance between our thoughts and feelings and thus, its involvement here supports how OM, as well as other meditative practices, can be useful in helping people regulate their emotions.

It is important to note that decreased parietal lobe activity is also commonly seen in intense spiritual experiences, specifically as it pertains to one's sense of self. We have considered before how the parietal lobe is involved in our sense of self. Decreased parietal lobe activity is associated with a decreased sense of self, a loss of the boundary between the self and the rest of the world, and profound experiences of oneness or unity. That people practicing OM have decreased parietal lobe activity is consistent with their feeling of oneness and connectedness with each other and the world. A participant described it as such:

> I feel very connected to God and have a sense of oneness. It is this feeling like everything is going to be OK. And everything is right just the way it is supposed to be. I feel connected to God in a strong way and also deeply connected to myself. It is like we are together in this world. And there is a sense of deep joy and gratitude for the world.

Two other areas of the brain that were found to be affected during OM are the insula and precuneus. The insula is a very important structure that lies between the limbic system and the outer layers of the cortex, and it is particularly involved in helping us perceive and understand the emotions we feel. The insula is critically important for empathy and social interactions with other people. In a similar manner, the precuneus is part of the parietal lobe and our social network in the brain. It helps us to establish our sense of self and how that self relates to other individuals around us. The fact that these two areas are particularly affected by the OM practice further validates the importance of this hybrid practice in creating a stronger social bond between participants. This also supports the evolutionary role of mating and spirituality since both ultimately lead to the bringing together of various members of a group.

It was also noted that a few parts of the temporal lobe had increased activity that is probably more related to the sexual stimulation part of the OM practice. But this is also an important finding as it helps bridge the connection between sexuality and spirituality. It does in fact appear that through sexual stimulation, and the intense focus during the practice, practitioners are able to induce powerful spiritual states.

This would make sense if sexuality and spirituality were tightly linked. In fact, our original research detailing the importance of rituals, and how they can bring two people together, a family together, or a society together, revealed the importance of these brain structures in both sexuality and spirituality.

Turning to specific differences between males and females, we also saw distinctions in relation to the OM practice. Females had changes in their brain similar to the entire group, including decreases in the frontal lobe, parietal lobe, insula, and precuneus. They also had decreases in the limbic areas, consistent with the feeling of relaxation and bliss in the midst of the hyperarousal state that accompanied an increase in parts of the frontal lobe.

Males had similar decreases in the frontal lobe, and some parts of the parietal lobe, but not to the same degree as the females. Interestingly, the males had an increase in a large structure at the base of the brain called the cerebellum. This increase probably reflected two important characteristics of the OM practice. The cerebellum is particularly involved in motor coordination, and hence during the OM practice, the coordinated movements of stroking the female clitoris probably had something to do with how the male cerebellum was working. Interestingly, the cerebellum is also involved in coordinating emotional responses, and so the increased activity in the cerebellum in the males probably had something to do with their emotional reactivity and coordination as well.

Overall, these findings demonstrate that males and females can experience different effects during the OM practice, a finding that makes sense given that they are doing related but different things during the practice. As previously stated, these findings directly link sexuality and spirituality, as the changes observed during the OM practice much more represent other spiritual practices rather than sexual excitement itself. In particular, decreased activity observed during OM was in areas that are part of the default mode network which is active during the resting state of the brain and has been shown to be decreased in other meditation practices.[63] Of course, there are some elements that are consistent with sexual excitement too, which goes even further to demonstrate the sexual-spiritual relationship.

MRI RESULTS TOO!

While we saw the aforementioned changes present in the PET scans, we also obtained MRI scans before and after doing the OM practice. The results were striking and are also relevant in the context of understanding the PET findings. With regard to the MRI scans, we specifically looked at changes in functional connectivity, which has to do with how different parts of the brain connect to each other and work together. In doing so, we noted there were significant differences between the pre- and post- OM scans, and importantly, the changes that we observed were in similar brain structures to those found during the PET scans. Thus, we concluded the OM practice is not only associated with metabolic changes but also with changes in how the brain regions connect with each other.

And perhaps even more important from a clinically oriented perspective is that since these changes in functional connectivity were observed *after* the OM practice was completed, it implies that these are changes that persist when the practice is over. This suggests that the practice may produce longer-term changes in brain function that could be useful in considering its potential clinical effects in helping people with problems such as depression or anxiety. But more about that in chapter 6. For now, it is consistent with our studies of many other spiritual practices that show changes during the practice itself but longer-term effects that can transform the individual.

---

63   Andrews-Hanna JR, Smallwood J, Spreng RN. The default network and self-generated thought: component processes, dynamic control, and clinical relevance. *Ann N Y Acad Sci.* 2014;1316(1):29-52.

In this regard, we can begin to connect how sexuality and spirituality lead to transformative changes in the brain. Powerful spiritual experiences or enlightenment experiences can represent the moment of enlightenment itself, but can also refer to the long-term state of the enlightened individual. Perhaps we were getting a glimpse of this as well.

CHAPTER 6

GOD MOLECULES AND
SEX MOLECULES

When emotions are expressed . . . all systems are united and made whole. When emotions are repressed, denied, not allowed to be whatever they may be, our network pathways get blocked, stopping the flow of the vital feel-good, unifying chemicals that run both our biology and our behavior.

—Candace B. Pert, *The Molecules of Emotion*

THE BASIS OF RELIGIOUS EVOLUTION

The studies we have been looking at so far have focused primarily on how different parts of the brain relate to both sexuality and spirituality. With our study of OM, we have seen how intricate this interrelationship can be. We have found at least part of the missing link that helps us tie mating rituals with spiritual rituals. But there are more than just "parts of the brain" that get involved with sexuality and spirituality. There is a more detailed problem about how various parts of the brain work and communicate with other parts of the brain. As it turns out, communication between parts of the brain, and specifically between nerve cells, occurs primarily through the use of a multitude of molecules, usually referred to as neurotransmitters. These molecules allow nerve cells to know what other nerve cells are doing. These molecules also tell other nerve cells what to do, usually either turning nerve cells on or off. And these molecules can often have very specific functions such as for cognition, emotion, sensation, movement, or pain. What is also amazing about these molecules is that many of them are evolutionarily ancient. They are found in the nervous system of almost all animal species.

Focusing on these molecules provides another basis for understanding how spirituality and religion may have evolved in humans. After all, evolutionary processes lead the brain to change in certain ways that may optimize some thought patterns and not others, or some emotions and not others. But how does this optimization occur? It is based on how different neurotransmitters work, how they are released, and how they are received. If we think about humans as creative, we can ask what neurotransmitters seem to lead to creativity. Similarly, if we think about humans as social, we can ask what neurotransmitters lead to increased social behaviors. And if we think about humans as spiritual, we can ponder what neurotransmitters lead to religious and spiritual experiences as well as beliefs.

As I have argued throughout this book, though, all of these molecules originate for the fundamental purpose of surviving and procreating. If those don't happen, the species becomes extinct. Species that have survived have nervous systems with neurotransmitter functions that work well. They are selected for by the processes of natural selection and sexual selection.

This latter point is quite important because it helps us to truly understand the evolutionary forces that led to human beings developing religion along with all of the highest aspects of human behaviors. This includes creativity, music, language, and ultimately civilization. I mentioned earlier in this book that there has never been a civilization that has arisen without some type of religious or spiritual foundation. But how and why would this common intersection of sexuality and spirituality be so important to the development of religion? We consider this issue briefly here, which then sets up our discussion about the molecules common to sexuality and spirituality.

A number of scholars have actually tried to clarify the forces that affect human evolution. We have mentioned previously that there are two main ways in which evolution occurs—survival advantage and sexual advantage. I have previously argued in *Why God Won't Go Away* that religion and spirituality support both types of adaptive processes.[64]

---

64   Newberg A, d'Aquili E, Rause V. *Why God Won't Go Away: Brain Science and the Biology of Belief.* Ballantine Books; 2001.

Religion and spirituality do this by connecting with two very basic functions of the brain, self-maintenance and self-transcendence, which in turn, relate to the two basic evolutionary processes. Self-maintenance has to do with how we maintain our livelihood. We need to be able to know what foods to eat, what predators to avoid, and for humans, how to create social groups that further support survival. Religion seems to be an excellent way of supporting self-maintenance.[65] Religions provide a sense of understanding about the world and how to interact with the world. This includes how we interact with the world on a large scale, like helping us interpret the seasons, knowing when to plant crops, and providing some sense of control over weather patterns. Religion also provides a set of morals by which we can develop interpersonal relationships and cohesive societies. Sacred texts are filled with information on how to develop relationships with loved ones such as spouses, children, the nuclear family, the broader family, and other members of society. By following these moral tenets, we can have a stable society that is generally supportive of its individual members.

Religion also helps foster personal survival through various practices that can include meditation or prayer that reduce anxiety and depression, beliefs that provide a sense of meaning and purpose, and even dietary habits that might lead to a healthier lifestyle. These individual behaviors have all been demonstrated in medical literature to provide substantial health benefits for individuals. In fact, religious and spiritual individuals have been shown to live longer than those without a faith tradition.[66] In this way, along with the more societal benefits, religious and spiritual beliefs and practices help to maintain the self effectively. Thus, religion and spirituality can certainly have evolved as a part of natural selection by making the person more adaptive for survival.

Religion may be unique within human beings in that it not only helps as an adaptive survival advantage but may also be sexually selective as well. What does this mean? A number of scholars have suggested the importance

---

65   Newberg A, d'Aquili E, Rause V. *Why God Won't Go Away: Brain Science and the Biology of Belief.* Ballantine Books; 2001.

66   Lucchetti G, Lucchetti AL, Koenig HG. Impact of spirituality/religiosity on mortality: comparison with other health interventions. *Explore.* 2011;7(4):234-238.

of sexual selection for the developing human mind. Sexual selection involves how human beings identify prospective mates. Since finding a mate that is likely to yield children with strong survival abilities is essential, nature is replete with many sexually selective adaptations. However, sexual selection on the surface often seems to be based more on personal preference than on adaptability. In fact, many ornaments that have developed over millions of years in various species may actually be disadvantages from a survival perspective. Because of their potential cost to the individual, they also signify survival adaptability because they allow the individual to demonstrate how fit they actually are that they can tolerate something which is potentially very detrimental to their survival.

Being able to sport large feathers or large racks of horns and antlers are not easy to maintain and require a great deal of muscular strength to be able to tolerate having them. But that also demonstrates to the female that a particular male is strong enough to be able to have such ornaments.

In human beings, physical ornaments appear to have given way to mental ones. Thinking about how human beings interact with each other and attract each other, we frequently talk about personality, talkativeness, or a sense of humor. In addition, human males had the ability to demonstrate personal commitment to the family, and personal resources such as providing food or shelter.[67] Each of these personal characteristics require large areas of the brain to be able to think in terms of language and humor, or to accumulate food and build a home. Thus, large areas of the brain had to evolve and had to evolve in a way that helped demonstrate the processes that they supported. As I have argued previously, males must adapt and evolve along with females. It is useless for a male to have a great sense of humor if the female can't recognize it. The male and female brain had to evolve in similar manners to support the explosion of cognitive and emotional processes that led to creativity, music, language, and a sense of humor.[68] These became elements of humanity that were exciting and enticing to explore for both males and females together.

Where might religion fit into all of this?

---

67 Buss DM. *Evolution of Desire: Strategies of Human Mating.* Basic Books; 2016.

68 Miller G. *The Mating Mind.* Anchor Books; 2001.

It turns out that religion also has a way of demonstrating the complex processes of the human mind. Practices like meditation and prayer require a great deal of mental control, understanding, and knowledge. Religion provides creative stories requiring advanced language skills that can fascinate us in terms of how we think about the world and how we understand it. Demonstrating such ideas and knowledge reflects a higher level of intelligence that comes with a survival advantage. And since religion and spiritual beliefs lead to societal groups that support each other, that important trait may have been very attractive to females who typically strive to create more cohesive social groups. Thus, religion provided value for both males and females.

There are other ways in which religion and spirituality may also demonstrate the power of the human mind. Religious beliefs create a sense of the absolute which may be helpful in understanding the whimsical nature of the world around us. After all, when it comes to social groups, there tend to be hierarchies that must be maintained. The hierarchical structure of mammals is essential for maintaining strong group cohesiveness. There are always leaders or "alpha males" or "queen bees." Religion in some sense provides the ultimate target of a leader which actually goes beyond humanity and is in the form of something or someone sacred such as God.

In this way, religion creates what is considered to be a "non-arbitrary" basis for the nature of the universe and how human beings are to behave. Of course, for anyone who doesn't agree with a given religion, the beliefs of that tradition are regarded as completely arbitrary, but for members of that spiritual community, all of the tenets are derived directly from God. Thus, the king is not a king because human beings say so. A king is a king because God says so.

THE MOLECULES OF EVOLUTION

Now that we have reviewed the basic argument about how spirituality arose from sexuality, we can consider in more detail how neurotransmitters are central to this evolutionary process. Neurotransmitter molecules produced by neurons provide neurons the ability to talk to each other.

Some neurotransmitters activate or turn on other neurons while other neurotransmitters inhibit or turn off other neurons. This overall push and pull enables the brain to function properly.

But where did neurotransmitters come from?

These are very ancient molecules that existed in almost all multicellular animals from the first amphibians, to reptiles, to mammals and ultimately humans. Thus, the same neurotransmitters running around your brain during sex were also running around the brain of *Machimosaurus*. Some of the well-known neurotransmitters are acetylcholine, glutamate, gamma amino butyric acid (GABA), dopamine, serotonin, and oxytocin. There are many others, but we will focus on these because they are the most important in the brain, and also the most important when it comes to sexuality and spirituality.

Let's start with acetylcholine. Not many people outside the medical world have heard about this brain molecule but it is the main excitatory neurotransmitter along with glutamate. They turn on neurons and so are used in the brain to get whole networks of neurons to fire together. Essentially, the brain would not work without acetylcholine and glutamate. While you probably haven't heard of acetylcholine, there are two types of acetylcholine receptors, one of which will sound very familiar: the muscarinic and nicotinic. Nicotinic receptors are named after and stimulated by the nicotine in tobacco, which is functionally similar to acetylcholine.

When a person is turned on sexually, acetylcholine is released throughout the brain in order to turn on various brain structures.[69] This increases our sense of arousal, increases our emotions, and increases our cognitive processes. While we don't know for sure, it would seem that there is a release of acetylcholine during peak spiritual practices. It might also not be a surprise that early religious ceremonies sometimes used tobacco as a stimulant to facilitate deep experiences.

Acetylcholine is also important in turning on the autonomic nervous

---

69   Calabrò RS, Cacciola A, Bruschetta D, et al. Neuroanatomy and function of human sexual behavior: a neglected or unknown issue? *Brain Behav.* 2019;9(12):e01389. doi:10.1002/brb3.1389.; Floody OR. Role of acetylcholine in control of sexual behavior of male and female mammals. *Pharmacol Biochem Behav.* 2014;120:50-56.

system and so it is intimately involved in how we are able to feel spiritual and sexual experiences throughout the body. It helps us feel the sense of arousal and ecstasy as well as the profound feeling of blissfulness. These are reflected in the many changes observed in heart rate, blood pressure, and other measures of the autonomic nervous system. And remember how the autonomic nervous system was affected during the OM practice. This supports the relationship between the evolution of the autonomic nervous system and how sexual and spiritual behaviors connect. They both make use of acetylcholine to turn on the arousal and quiescent systems of the body.

The next neurotransmitter to consider is GABA, which is the counter to acetylcholine and glutamate, and is the primary inhibitory neurotransmitter in the brain. GABA may be crucial to the sense of oneness and sense of surrender frequently associated with both sexual and spiritual experiences. How might this happen?

Remember that the sense of oneness or unity is associated with decreased activity in the parietal lobes. As the parietal lobes shut down, the sense of self that they help support fades away. We lose our sense of self, experience the blurring of the boundary between ourselves and others, and ultimately feel a sense of oneness or connectedness. But what shuts the parietal lobe down? It is likely to be GABA. In fact, research studies have shown an increase in GABA in the brain during intense meditation practices.[70] This is associated with the sense of oneness but also the more general sense of relaxation. Furthermore, medications that act on the GABA system have primarily antianxiety effects. Such medications are used to relax people for surgery, or are given to reduce anxiety symptoms in patients with post-traumatic stress disorder (PTSD) or generalized anxiety disorder. The profound sense of blissfulness during spiritual practices is likely associated with the release of GABA.

Finally, GABA can help inhibit frontal lobe activity, and when that happens, we lose our sense of willfulness and purposefulness. We feel as if we surrender ourselves or are taken over by some external force.

If all this sounds familiar, it should.

---

70   Streeter CC, Jensen JE, Perlmutter RM, et al. Yoga asana sessions increase brain GABA levels: a pilot study. *J Altern Complement Med.* 2007;13(4):419-426.

Sexual orgasm is usually associated with the powerful sense of oneness with your mate (decreased parietal lobe). And during orgasm, you feel as if you are no longer in charge of what is going on (decreased frontal lobe). It happens automatically, and you are along for the ride—literally. Eventually you are overcome with deep blissfulness, which is the GABA working on your primary emotional centers. Thus, GABA is a potent neurotransmitter involved with both intense spiritual and sexual experiences.

The next neurotransmitter of interest is dopamine. Dopamine is often called the "feel good" molecule and is part of the brain's reward system.[71] A release of dopamine is associated with strong feelings of arousal, and particularly joy and euphoria. The best-known example of this is when someone uses cocaine. Cocaine causes the brain to become highly sensitive to dopamine, essentially resulting in a flood of dopamine that is associated with the intense emotional high. As the cocaine leaves the brain, dopamine levels drop and the high goes away. If a person continues to use cocaine, the brain becomes sensitized, needing more and more cocaine to reach the same level of feeling, and hence, more dopamine to produce the feeling. This is why people become so easily addicted.

Studies have shown that dopamine is released during spiritual practices such as meditation.[72] This might help to explain why people can have intensely positive emotions of joy or ecstasy. We have previously studied this during an immersive one-week spiritual retreat on the dopamine system. After a week of intense meditation, prayer, and personal reflection, we found that the brain had become sensitized to the effects of dopamine, much like the effects of cocaine.[73] And it will likely not be a surprise to learn that do-

---

71   Arias-Carrión O, Stamelou M, Murillo-Rodríguez E, Menéndez-González M, Pöppel E. Dopaminergic reward system: a short integrative review. *Int Arch Med.* 2010;3:24. doi:10.1186/1755-7682-3-24.

72   Kjaer TW, Bertelsen C, Piccini P, Brooks D, Alving J, Lou HC. Increased dopamine tone during meditation-induced change of consciousness. *Brain Res Cogn Brain Res.* 2002;13(2):255-259.

73   Newberg AB, Wintering N, Yaden DB, et al. Effect of a one-week spiritual retreat on dopamine and serotonin transporter binding: a preliminary study. *Religion Brain Behav.* 2017. doi:10.1080/2153599X.2016.1267035.

pamine is released during sexual orgasm as well.[74] Thus, we see the powerful effect of spirituality building off of the dopamine system that was in place millions of years ago to help us find sex and orgasm a fun thing to do.

Serotonin is similar to dopamine structurally and is a powerful modulator of mood and sensation. Drugs such as LSD and psilocybin particularly affect the serotonin system, producing psychedelic effects that stretch the mind and senses. An increasing number of research studies have shown that drugs such as psilocybin produce experiences typically referred to as spiritual.[75] In our Survey of Spiritual Experiences, we directly compared experiences associated with psychedelic drugs to those occurring through more natural, spiritual processes. The results demonstrated great similarity in terms of the degree of spirituality and the ways in which people described these experiences. In fact, our study showed that experiences induced by psychedelic substances were rated as more mystical and spiritual, and increased the person's sense of purpose in life and reduced their fear of death, compared to nonpsychedelically triggered spiritual experiences. These findings lend support to the idea that psychedelic substances can enable people to have mystical experiences with generally positive outcomes.

Sexuality has also been associated with serotonin release. In fact, some studies have documented that increasing sexual frequency can help reduce anxiety and depression.[76] Furthermore, in our retreat study, we found that intense spiritual practices potentiate the effect of serotonin much like the effects of various psychedelic compounds.

74　Argiolas A, Melis MR. The neurophysiology of the sexual cycle. *J Endocrinol Invest.* 2003;26(3 Suppl):20-22.

75　Yaden DB, Nguyen KDL, Kern ML, et al. Of roots and fruits: a comparison of psychedelic and non-psychedelic mystical experiences. *J Human Psychol.* 2016;57(4):338-353; Griffiths RR, Hurwitz ES, Davis AK, Johnson MW, Jesse R. Survey of subjective "God encounter experiences": comparisons among naturally occurring experiences and those occasioned by the classic psychedelics psilocybin, LSD, ayahuasca, or DMT. *PLoS One.* 2019;14(4):e0214377. doi:10.1371/journal.pone.0214377.

76　Mollaioli D, Sansone A, Ciocca G, et al. Benefits of sexual activity on psychological, relational, and sexual health during the COVID-19 breakout. *J Sex Med.* 2021. doi: 10.1016/j.jsxm.2020.10.008.

It also makes sense that psychedelics such as LSD or psilocybin, which both operate primarily on the serotonin system, seem to reduce sexual inhibition and increase sexual behaviors. Some people have even reported becoming nymphomaniacs.[77] Again, that these different types of experiences—psychedelic, sexual, and spiritual—all interconnect when it comes to the effects of serotonin, shows how they co-evolved together.

The final neurotransmitter to discuss is oxytocin. Oxytocin is released at two main life events—sexual orgasm and childbirth. Thus, oxytocin helps bind two people together. In the case of sex, it brings you and your mate together for pair bonding. This establishes two people as mates and also supports the evolution of sexual selection. This latter point is important. If members of a species simply mated with any individual, there would be no need for sexual selection. It would all proceed willy-nilly and only the strongest sperm and egg would produce offspring. Other external forces would not be involved. When you are required to select a specific mate then sexual selection begins to take hold. If you are only going to mate with one or a few other individuals, you had better make sure they are good ones. Thus, oxytocin is a critical player when it comes to evolution through its influence on sexual selection.

Perhaps the most notable example of oxytocin's effects is in a small animal called a prairie vole.[78] The prairie voles are small rodents that have several subspecies. One of the subspecies is completely monogamous, mating with their partners for life. The other subspecies is highly promiscuous, mating with any acceptable prairie vole they come across. But why would two genetically similar species seem to act so differently? The answer, it was found, is oxytocin. The monogamous prairie voles have a brain that is loaded with oxytocin. The promiscuous ones have very little oxytocin and have a different neurotransmitter—called vasopressin—present in their

---

77   Dymock A. Acid and Orgasms: Why LSD Failed to Sexually Liberate Women. Chacruna Institute for Psychedelic Plant Medicines. 2020. Accessed March 23, 2023. https://chacruna.net/why-lsd-sex-failed-to-liberate-women/.

78   Young KA, Liu Y, Wang Z. The neurobiology of social attachment: a comparative approach to behavioral, neuroanatomical, and neurochemical studies. *Comp Biochem Physiol C Toxicol Pharmacol.* 2008;148(4):401-410.

brain. Thus, prairie voles help to demonstrate the powerful relationship between the approach to sexuality and the brain. Perhaps human beings share similar capacities to connect or be promiscuous. Given the human history of social bonding, it certainly seems that connecting with one or a few individuals is far more common. Even in indigenous cultures that involve mating with multiple partners, they are almost always within the society so that there is still an overall sense of connectedness, just expanded beyond the traditional pair bond.

The role of oxytocin in childbirth is also quite important in bonding the mother to the infant. This is essential for species survival. However, it should also be noted that in spiritual and religious circles, birth is a primal concept that connects people to a creator. The creator could be God, consciousness, or nature itself, but there is a profound sense of connection between us and whatever created us. Thus, one of the primary tenets of virtually every religion is based on the creative process of sex and childbirth— tying all of this once again to spirituality and sexuality.

Oxytocin has also been shown to be involved with meditation practices, especially those that support feelings of empathy and compassion. Since meditation is associated with profound experiences of oneness and connectedness, oxytocin is likely a prominent player in supporting those feelings. Since oxytocin is involved in bringing animals and people together for mating, it makes sense that it would be similarly involved in connecting people to larger societies, all of humanity, the universe, or God. Spirituality might be viewed as the ultimate expression of oxytocin which has evolved in so many animals, and especially human beings.

There is a plethora of additional neurotransmitters that are also involved in sexuality and spirituality, and far too many to mention within the confines of this book. However, one that is frequently part of the conversation are opiates. Opiates such as morphine or heroin have profound effects on the brain. And while they produce a kind of euphoria, the research on their connection with sexuality and spirituality is much less clear. However, our models of spiritual practices and experiences do consider how all of the neurotransmitter systems might become involved.

Suffice it to say here that we can now see how the connection in the brain between sexuality and spirituality runs very deep. It is not just about brain networks and the different structures that support those networks. It arises at the molecular level of the neurotransmitters and how the brain works at a very basic, even primitive level. The primitive nature of this interaction, with so many of the sexual neurotransmitters occurring in animals that are hundreds of millions of years old, only helps to further support how the evolution of these neurotransmitters and brain functions corresponds with the evolution of human spirituality.

CHAPTER 7

THE SPIRITUAL
BRAIN ON DRUGS

I believe that all hallucinogenic substances are here for the use of transcendence. God created these things for us to find so that we may better understand that we do not know nearly as much as we think we do. These experiences are profound. I saw the universe. I came to cosmic realizations that I cannot possibly describe.

—Subject from our Survey of Spiritual Experiences describing
hallucinogenic experiences

NEUROTRANSMITTERS, DRUGS, AND SPIRITUALITY

In the previous chapter, we considered the relationship between sexuality and spirituality from the perspective of different neurotransmitters. These neurotransmitters evolved in animals and ultimately in humans as a way to facilitate the brain's functions. But these neurotransmitters were mostly developed for mating. They foster the mating rituals and produce the craving and desire for sex so animals continue to mate and generate subsequent generations.

But if the neurotransmitters are associated with cravings and ecstasy, then drugs that activate these neurotransmitter systems are likely to do the same thing. That is why drugs are associated with cravings and why they stimulate intense experiences that are often regarded as spiritual. The exploding field of psychedelic research supports these very contentions and speaks to the people who share the same perspective, such as the person whose quote opens this chapter. But we can look more deeply into how drugs, the brain, sex, and spirituality all interconnect. In fact, it should not be surprising that many substances such as magic mushrooms or ayahuasca have been used for millennia to facilitate spiritual experiences, particularly in Shamanic cultures.

When we talk about the brain on drugs in the context of sexuality and spirituality, the overall puzzle appears to become clearer still. And the implications of this knowledge are widespread both in terms of realizing the relationship between spirituality and sexuality, as well as more directly engaging ways of helping people deal with a wide variety of mental health issues.

With regard to the latter, we shall see that drugs, spirituality, and sexuality all have the potential to be useful in helping people deal with mental illnesses such as depression and anxiety. In fact, research has shown that each of these approaches, when studied individually, has been beneficial in a number of patient populations.

Prescription antidepressants, antianxiety, and antipsychotic medications have all been used to help people with a variety of mental health problems. Importantly, these prescribed medications are known to affect specific neurotransmitter systems.

Antidepressant medications have typically involved molecules that modify the brain's serotonin system.[79] Early antidepressants, called monoamine oxidase inhibitors, enabled the brain to maintain higher levels of serotonin and dopamine. Around the year 1990, drugs such as Prozac and Zoloft became available because they blocked the serotonin reuptake sites on neurons. Reuptake sites typically clear the brain of excess serotonin so that it can be recycled. By blocking these reuptake sites, more serotonin was available in the brain. Over time, these drugs help to reduce depressive symptoms and improve outcomes.

Of course, these medications also have a variety of side effects. One of the most common side effects with regard to antidepressant medications is decreased sexual desire and function. The impact on sexual function

---

79   Preskorn SH, Ross R, Stanga CY. Selective serotonin reuptake inhibitors. In: Preskorn SH, Feighner HP, Stanga CY, Ross R, eds. *Antidepressants: Past, Present and Future.* Springer; 2004:241-262.

is one of the primary reasons that people stop using these medications. Hence, we can see a relationship between serotonin, depression, and sexuality. However, the relationship seems complex because the serotonin system is being modified over longer periods of time. A very different situation arises when serotonin is affected quickly and robustly. Psychedelic compounds such as LSD and psilocybin cause profound stimulation of the serotonin receptors that produce powerful experiences that we have considered previously but which are increasingly explored for having therapeutic effects.

More recently, it has been realized that other neurotransmitter systems are also likely involved with depression, which has led to the development of medications affecting multiple neurotransmitter systems.[80] Our models of spiritual practices similarly suggest that there are multiple neurotransmitter systems that are involved. Therefore, we can see that there may be a direct relationship between a complex network of neurotransmitters that are associated with overall mental health and well-being.

Another player in this regard are medications that affect the GABA receptor system. These popular prescription drugs, typically referred to as benzodiazepines, include Valium, Ativan, and Xanax. Each is designed to stimulate the GABA receptors, which are the primary inhibitory neurotransmitters in the brain. Stimulation of these receptors shuts down neurons, and hence, decreases activity in different parts of the brain, particularly its emotional centers. Since anxiety and stress increases brain activity as it becomes hypervigilant and hyperexcited, GABA medicines calm the brain down, literally and psychologically.

Studies have shown that practices such as meditation and prayer similarly cause an increase in GABA, which likely leads to the stress-reducing qualities of these practices.[81] These practices have also been used to reduce

80   Andrade C, Rao NS. How antidepressant drugs act: a primer on neuroplasticity as the eventual mediator of antidepressant efficacy. *Indian J Psychiatry.* 2010;52(4):378-386.

81   Streeter CC, Jensen JE, Perlmutter RM, et al. Yoga asana sessions increase brain GABA levels: a pilot study. *J Altern Complement Med.* 2007;13(4):419-426.

anxiety and even post-traumatic stress disorder.[82] All of these psychological issues have the similar symptom of an overactive brain both cognitively and emotionally. Meditation and prayer, just like antianxiety medications, can be useful in helping to quiet the mind down.

Studies are also beginning to show how the combination of drugs, spiritual practices, and psychotherapy can synergistically help people with various mental health problems. The issue is that each of these approaches, while all affecting similar brain systems, do so differently. If you have traumas in your life, taking an antianxiety medication might reduce your reactivity to those traumas, but does not remove them. Psychotherapy can help you to better cope with those traumas, but it might not be effective if you are so overreactive that you can't even talk about them in the first place. And many times, people suffering from anxiety and depression look at religion or spirituality in negative ways. Some people even think that God is punishing them, or at least not on their side. Consider the following interesting statement made by one of our survey participants:

> When I was beginning my college career, I experienced a significant episode of clinical depression, which effectively destroyed my previous spiritual worldview. What undermined my religious beliefs was the very lack of a religious experience during my depression—I would spend hours praying for relief from sadness and anxiety, expecting God to take away my pain. As my depression persisted, I saw the lack of direct religious experience vis-a-vis healing as a proof that God did not exist, and I essentially became an atheist.

A combination of these approaches might ultimately work the best. Perhaps a person needs some meditation just to keep the mind less active so that it can focus on the traumas and how they have affected them. Meditation can help reduce the reactivity while also opening up the mind to discussing and processing the different traumas. And then psychotherapeutic

---

82   Chen B, Yang T, Xiao L, Xu C, Zhu C. Effects of mobile mindfulness meditation on the mental health of university students: systematic review and meta-analysis. *J Med Internet Res.* 2023;25:e39128. doi:10.2196/39128.

approaches can help people more formally work through their traumas to get them into a better perspective on life. Helping a spiritual person embrace a positive outlook on the world or on God can similarly be beneficial in managing their mental health.

We have also previously described how an increase of GABA can be important for decreasing brain activity in structures such as the frontal and parietal lobes that appear to be particularly involved in spiritual experiences. Thus, decreased frontal lobe activity appears to be associated with a sense of surrender or letting go, while decreased parietal lobe activity appears to be associated with the loss of the sense of self and the sense of spacelessness or oneness.

In the end, an integrative model of mental health might be the most effective since it takes into consideration the broader link between the biological evolution of the brain with sexual and spiritual experiences to help people maintain their optimal brain health balance.

PSYCHEDELICS AND MENTAL HEALTH

In our Survey of Spiritual Experiences, we compared several hundred experiences that occurred under the influence of a psychedelic drug compared to more naturally occurring experiences and found a great deal of similarities in terms of how they were described. They also both have similar life-changing consequences. These types of experiences are described by individuals as the most intense experiences of their entire lives and can radically transform how they think about themselves and the world around them.

For these reasons, psychedelic drugs have become a hot-ticket item for exploring how they may help mental health problems. Ongoing research has shown that just one or two doses of a psychedelic drug can greatly reduce feelings of depression or PTSD.[83] One of our survey participants who

---

83   Mitchell JM, Bogenschutz M, Lilienstein A, et al. MDMA-assisted therapy for severe PTSD: a randomized, double-blind, placebo-controlled phase 3 study. *Nat Med.* 2021;27(6):1025-1033.

had found multiple forms of traditional antidepressants to have no therapeutic effect attributed their recovery from depression to the use of psychedelics on four separate occasions, taken in close proximity:

> The psychedelics showed me that I was lovable, wonderful, and a
> unique life form. All the shame, guilt, and terror melted away and
> I was left refreshed and at peace with life. I fully credit my psyche-
> delic experiences for helping me work through the traumas and get
> over my neurosis and mental illnesses.

The current studies of psychedelics are being expanded to explore the
utility and safety of these medications in a variety of psychiatric populations. Although these drugs seem to have therapeutic relevance, they are
often limited because of their blanketing effect on the brain. This means
the drugs do not target a specific area of the brain but rather all areas of the
brain at once. While this can sometimes be beneficial, it can also result in a
variety of undesired side effects.

While sometimes lauded as significantly impactful, research has shown
that the use of psychedelic drugs by themselves may not be fully sufficient,
since context and adjunct psychological support have proven beneficial to
providing a safe environment and appropriate direction for helping people transform themselves for the better. For instance, taking a psychedelic
drug at a college party is not likely to yield a therapeutic effect. But when
given under proper guidance, care, and support, these drugs and their con-
comitant experiences may be very therapeutic.

On the other hand, it might be argued that a safer therapeutic approach
would be through the use of spiritual practices that can elicit similar experiences, some of which have been shown to reduce depression and anxiety in a
variety of patient populations. An early study we performed found that engaging in a simple spiritual practice, such as the rosary, had significant effects
on reducing anxiety. Of course, context is extremely important when considering religious and spiritual practices. For instance, suggesting that a Jewish
person engage in a rosary practice because a study suggested use of a rosary
could be beneficial for reducing anxiety would not be likely to prove beneficial to the individual. A religious or spiritual practice only has the potential

to be beneficial if you believe in them and can be fully engaged in them. In fact, our studies have documented that when you perform a spiritual practice such as prayer in a very automatic manner, it can affect the brain a little bit and reduce anxiety and stress in a similarly small amount. However, when you are doing the practices with great authenticity and fervor, you will affect the brain a great deal. This can have important practical and clinical applications as it pertains to spirituality, sexuality, and the brain.

Research on Orgasmic Meditation, which incorporates sexuality into spirituality, suggests that it might be particularly useful at reducing a variety of psychological symptoms, particularly depression and anxiety.[84] In fact, our brain scan studies have shown that long term OM practitioners have different patterns of brain activity, particularly in cognitive and emotional centers, versus nonmeditators. Thus, it can be deduced there are possibly long-term neurophysiological effects of OM that may be associated with changes in mental health as well. Other mind-body practices, such as mindfulness, Transcendental Meditation, yoga, and many more, have been evaluated and almost all of them show some beneficial effect in the right setting. The problem at the moment is that we don't know which mind-body practices work best under which conditions. We don't know if some work better for older people, for men versus women, for people with depression versus anxiety. These are important questions that are starting to be evaluated.

DOPAMINE DRUGS AND THE BRAIN

The final type of drug to be mentioned in the moment are the ones that affect the dopamine system. On one hand, the dopamine parts of the brain are essential for the "reward system" that makes us feel happy. Dopamine

---

84   Prause N, Siegle GJ, Coan J. Partner intimate touch is associated with increased interpersonal closeness, especially in non-romantic partners. *PLoS One.* 2021;16(3):e0246065. doi:10.1371/journal.pone.0246065; Siegle GJ, Prause N. Intense positive affect without arousal is possible: subjective and physiological reactivity during a partnered sexual meditative experience. *Int J Psychophysiol.* 2022;178:99-107.

is released during positive emotions, and some drugs—such as cocaine—produce a significant influx of dopamine, thus causing powerful feelings of euphoria. Dopamine makes us happy, but too much or too little can be a problem. Too much dopamine can cause hallucinations and too little can cause depression or interfere with cognition. For these reasons, the dopamine system is frequently the target of antipsychotic medications, but it is also the target for prescription drugs for conditions such as attention deficit hyperactivity disorder (ADHD) and Parkinson's disease. Medications that reduce the effects of dopamine are particularly used for patients with schizophrenia or delirium as a way of helping to reduce hallucinations and delusions, by reducing the activity in the dopamine areas of the brain. However, individuals experiencing cognitive and emotional issues sometimes require medications that increase dopamine in the brain.

In terms of drugs that incur spiritual-like experiences, the most well-known is the euphoria associated with cocaine. Cocaine blocks the dopamine transporter which causes a flood of dopamine in the brain and the incredible high that people feel. There are a few studies that have shown that practices like meditation and prayer also cause a release of dopamine in the brain. One PET scan study specifically revealed such a release of dopamine in highly experienced Yoga Nidra meditators.[85]

Dopamine is also essential for romantic love, and it has been argued that the ability to form romantic bonds enables mate choice, which also makes the mating process more efficient.[86] Once you have identified your mate, you can help to guarantee your genetics will be part of future generations.

Dopamine is part of the initial state of sexual arousal and motivation and is fundamentally important for sexual intercourse and orgasm in both men and women. As previously mentioned in the last chapter, our research

---

85   Kjaer TW, Bertelsen C, Piccini P, Brooks D, Alving J, Lou HC. Increased dopamine tone during meditation-induced change of consciousness. *Brain Res Cogn Brain Res.* 2002;13(2):255-259.

86   Fisher H, Aron A, Brown LL. Romantic love: an fMRI study of a neural mechanism for mate choice. *J Comp Neurol.* 2005;493(1):58-62.

Amen D. *The Brain in Love.* Three Rivers Press, 2007.

study of an intense, immersive spiritual retreat documented a shift in the brain's sensitivity to dopamine as a result of a weeklong practice of meditation, self-reflection, and prayer. Thus, spiritual and sexual experiences both rely heavily on dopamine, again, another ancient neurotransmitter that exists in animals going back hundreds of millions of years.

The fascinating mental health interrelationships between sexuality, spirituality, and various drugs show how their underlying systems in the brain are closely related to each other and are highly interactive. It should make sense, then, that spirituality and sexuality have evolved together, and that various drugs can tweak these systems to induce a variety of neurological and psychological effects.

PART III

THE IMPACT OF THE CONNECTION—THE GOOD AND THE BAD

CHAPTER 8

SEXUAL AND SPIRITUAL ADDICTIONS

All I have done is by Our Lord's command. . . . I have done nothing in the world but by the order of God.

Act, and God will act.

—Joan of Arc

THE HYPER-RELIGIOUSNESS OF JOAN OF ARC

At 13 years old, she had visions of the archangel Michael, Margaret of Antioch, and Catherine of Alexander, all saints who told her to save France from the English. These visions made her deeply religious to the point where she was able to convince King Charles VII of France of her profound devotion and purity. She was even examined by a counsel of theologians who declared her to be a good Catholic, although they could not confirm the source of her visions. Due to her religious fervor and deep loyalty to her home country, France, she became a unique military leader who helped lead France in victory during the Hundred Years' War.

When she was eventually captured, she was put on trial and executed in part due to heresy because of the nature of her visions and her undying devotion to them. Her visions apparently told her to wear men's clothing as well as to fight her battles. She was unrepentant during her trial and subsequent execution, continually upholding and testifying to the intense religious nature of her experiences.

What do we make of someone like Joan of Arc? Clearly, she had unusual experiences. But these also led her to an intensity of religious following that may be unparalleled. Of course, many people follow religious beliefs to incredibly intense levels. Almost all saints certainly have. But what about monks, nuns, imams, rabbis, pastors, ministers, and priests? Each has committed their life to following their religion to an intense and relatively extreme degree, and in many cases, they withdraw from what would be considered standard everyday lifestyles. Priests and nuns do not marry or have children. Monks may spend many decades in a monastery in meditation. Most of them give up all worldly possessions. So, what can we say of such individuals?

We generally have the understanding that too much of anything, even a good thing, is ultimately a problem. The same is true with sex and religion. Or is it? Certainly, a healthy interest in sex is important in overall well-being and has an important evolutionary basis. However, if it becomes uncontrollable, or perverted, then it can result in serious crimes such as sexual abuse or rape.

The same may be true where religion is concerned. Religion appears to be generally beneficial, from a physical and mental health perspective, but there is reason for concern when a person becomes hyper-religious. In the case of mania or schizophrenia, hyper-religiousness can result in bizarre and maladaptive behaviors and obsessions. We have all heard of the schizophrenic patient who believes they are the messiah. On the other hand, a priest or nun who devotes their life to God is not considered a misfit, but is instead highly regarded within the tradition. They are considered to be wise, and their advice is greatly sought after, even for everyday things that they personally have no experience with, such as raising children. What can we make of our reliance, craving, and possibly addiction to sex and religion? Are these feelings the same or different, and are some better or worse?

Is there a degree or amount of religiousness enough to be regarded as an addiction? In some sense, it can be regarded as an addiction for hyper-religious people. It is something they do every day of their life. They would likely experience a kind of withdrawal becoming agitated or irritable if they could not engage in their religious beliefs, and they frequently do not act in the typical, adaptive manner in society. Of course, there are characteristics of other addictive disorders, such as substance abuse or alcoholism, that do not match the highly religious. In particular, highly religious individuals will not typically lie about the amount of engagement they have with their religion. Substance abusers often will not be honest with their friends and family about their addiction. Perhaps most importantly, substance addictions are typically acknowledged by the individual as being problematic, whereas being hyper-religious is regarded as a good thing by a highly religious individual and is something about which they are proud. In spite of this difference, there are a great deal of similarities between hyper-religious activities and addictions.[87]

As mentioned in the previous chapter on neurotransmitters, spiritual practices such as meditation and prayer can affect dopamine levels, and possibly the opiate system, both of which are highly implicated in addictive disorders. But since the exceedingly religious individual sees their lifestyle as being highly moral and appropriate, we might ask if this distinction is purely conceptual, or does it have something to do with brain chemistry? Most likely the answer is yes to both.

HYPER-RELIGIOUSNESS AND RITUALS

What is perhaps a unique distinction between the hyper-religious and those facing various addictions is the way in which the relevant rituals are engaged. In people with addictions, there are rituals associated with the use of the particular substance they take. An alcoholic might enjoy going to the local bar at the same time each night, saying "hello" to the fellow patrons, having their particular drinks in a particular order, and then leaving for home. However, the substance abuser will likely not incorporate the substance rituals into everyday life. Everyday life is kept distinct, at least to some extent.

For the hyper-religious individual, the religious rituals do not occur only in a special place such as a church or mosque, they occur throughout virtually every phase of their life. Deeply religious individuals make religion the centerpiece of their life. For example, an orthodox Jew will

---

87   Pearson RS. *Hyperreligiosity: Identifying and Overcoming Patterns of Religious Dysfunction*. Telical Books; 2005.

say prayers throughout the day, will arrange their diet to follow the laws of Kosher, and will follow the Sabbath by not doing anything—no driving, telephoning, or use of anything mechanical, and certainly no working. Religion enhances their life by connecting each component to a higher meaning. Getting up in the morning is not just getting up, but is part of the process of thanking God for the morning and for being alive. Prayers are said at each meal to bless the food and make it sacred. Life rituals for birth, growing up, marrying, and dying are also part of the religious approach and sanctify each of these stages of life. It is this latter element of "self-transcendence" that is a particularly powerful part of religion. It helps us move from one stage of life to the next. And perhaps religion even provides a way to advance toward a higher consciousness or enlightenment.

Unlike hyper-religiousness, substance abuse virtually never advances the person, but rather it usually interferes with everyday life and can sometimes bring that life crashing down. When that happens, meaning and purpose in life is lost which is why turning to religious and spiritual beliefs can sometimes be the only way out. It is the proverbial "hitting rock bottom" that induces the person to find another way.

CULTS, RITUALS, AND SEXUALITY

For the substance abuser, switching to a spiritual path frequently is a way to improve one's life and find meaning and purpose in life. However, there are times when the spiritual path becomes just as destructive as the path toward substance addiction.[88] Cults are a particularly well-known example of such an occurrence. When people enter into a cult, they are usually looking for direction, meaning, and purpose in their life. Traditional routes seem to have fallen short. Typically, a charismatic leader sells the person on the

---

88   Minor RN. *When Religion is an Addiction.* HumanityWorks!; 2007; Pearson RS. *Hyperreligiosity: Identifying and Overcoming Patterns of Religious Dysfunction.* Telical Books; 2005; Promises Behavioral Health / Behavioral Addiction. Can Religion Be an Addiction? Promises Behavioral Health. 2013. Accessed March 17, 2023. https://www.promises.com/addiction-blog/can-religion-be-an-addiction/.

ideas of the cult and then the rituals take over by deeply connecting the person to the cult, the ideas of the cult, and most importantly, the leader. After a period of time, the rituals have rewired the brain so that the cult is the only thing the person sees as being true or real. They can follow the cult to a potentially deadly end. There are many historical examples of this occurring, such as in the instance of the Jonestown massacre or the Heaven's Gate mass suicide (where those present believed a spaceship was coming with the Hale-Bopp comet).

Interestingly, cults are frequently associated with unusual sexual behaviors or rituals. Cults are often associated with the exploitation of vulnerable individuals through the use of manipulative and coercive techniques. One of the ways in which cult leaders may exert control over their followers is through the use of sexuality. Cult leaders may present themselves as having divine or supernatural powers and may use this to justify their sexual relationships with followers, somewhat akin to the sacred prostitutes previously discussed in the context of ancient civilizations.[89] These relationships can be particularly damaging given the power imbalance that exists between the cult leader and their followers. Cult leaders may also use these relationships to keep their followers dependent on them and to prevent them from leaving the group.

Thus, cults may use sexual practices or rituals as a means of controlling the cult members.[90] These practices may be presented as being spiritually or morally beneficial and may be used to encourage members to conform to the beliefs and practices of the group. Such rituals can bind a group together and also signal commitment to the group. However, these practices may also be physically or psychologically harmful or exploitative and may leave members feeling violated or traumatized. The use of sexuality in cults can have profoundly detrimental effects on the individuals involved. Individuals who have been victimized may experience shame, guilt, and a sense of betrayal and may struggle to trust others in the future. Additionally, the

---

89 Lalich J. *Bounded Choice: True Believers and Charismatic Cults*. University of California Press; 2004.

90 Katchen JE, Popper M. Cult-related sexual abuse: a systematic review. *J Child Sex Abuse*. 2019;28(8):919-937.

damage caused by cults can extend beyond the individual level, impacting families and communities as a whole.

It is important to recognize the ways in which cults may use sexuality to manipulate and control their members and to take steps to prevent and respond to instances of abuse or exploitation. This may involve increasing awareness and education around the issue, as well as providing support and resources for individuals who have been victimized. It may also be useful to evaluate brain scans of cult members, especially those who have been the recipients of sexual abuse, to determine whether there are changes that are similar to other people who have suffered sexual abuse or whether there are unique findings that characterize the effects of cults on the brain.

One additionally interesting note, related to the Orgasmic Meditation program that we have discussed in previous chapters regarding its neurophysiology, is that some people have accused the OM group as being "cult-like." Some of the rituals and programs that were initially offered by the main OM people were designed to create a cohesive and inclusive group of individuals. Given the sexual nature of OM, trying to develop a strong sense of trust and connectedness among people who are engaged in this practice is likely to be very important. But doing this can also lead to people feeling coerced or shunned, depending on how they respond to the overall group dynamics.

In a similar manner, people in various religious groups can feel the same way. There are many stories of people losing their family and friends when they leave a church or other religious group. Clearly there is a balance that needs to be struck between creating a strong social network that is supportive and positive versus one that becomes destructive and negative. Further, there are always going to be those individuals that either fit in well, or don't fit in, leading to disgruntled feelings about a given group. For example, many people found the OM practice and OM group very welcoming and positive, while others felt the group was highly problematic.

From the perspective of the brain, we can ponder how people that lead a given spiritual group, and people who take part in that group, respond to each other and the various elements that define that group. In my prior work, I discussed the basis for the in-group versus out-group system of beliefs. The decrease in parietal lobe function facilitates a person feeling at one with, or connected with, a specific group or idea. This fosters intense positive feelings with other members of the group, especially when they are embedded with various rituals that further connect the group by tugging on the brain's social areas. However, Gene d'Aquili and I frequently stated that "rituals are a morally neutral technology" and, therefore, leaders can also use those rituals to become exclusive and destructive toward anyone that is not in that group, and particularly for those who want to leave the group. Thus, for the leaders who strongly believe in the group and the ideals around which the group arises, the result can be either highly positive or negative, both for themselves as well as for the participants.

For participants that enjoy the group and feel deeply included, this can lead to very positive feelings both for other members of the group as well as for the health and well-being of the individual. However, for those individuals who do not want to participate in the group, they can frequently feel oppressed and threatened by members of the group. This can trigger a fight, flight, freeze, or fawn response in the person who does not fit in, and ultimately result in a traumatic separation from the group. Such has certainly been the case with the OM group, and it represents a fascinating opportunity to consider how these types of groups form, maintain themselves, and disperse. It also raises questions about how certain groups are able to maintain themselves over long periods of time similar to the primary religious traditions of today. At the beginning, they were all small groups, sometimes considered cults, but eventually their members and belief system grew and strengthened. This was possibly because there was something about those belief systems that had a broad effect on the brains of increasingly larger populations of people.

BALANCING BELIEFS

If one were to take a completely neutral viewpoint, it could be argued that members of cults are following a belief in something more important than the norms of everyday life. In a similar manner, a nun or monk forgoes the normal everyday life as well, following their intense religious beliefs. However, the latter is generally not destructive and not something that causes distress. On the other hand, history is replete with examples of people killed because of their beliefs, such as early Christians, who were frequently martyred due to their personal experiences and religious beliefs. One might argue that these sacrifices were poor choices on the part of the individual, but many of these individuals were ultimately regarded as spiritual leaders or saints. They advanced the religion, and today, Christianity has over two billion followers. So, is the difference between a hyper-religious person today and a hyper-religious Christian in the third century just a matter of timing and success regarding their tradition? From a historical perspective, as the saying goes, history is written by the victors. If the Catholic Church is still around and doing well, then their martyrs might be regarded as saints, whereas the followers of other traditions that have fallen by the wayside are likely to be regarded as heretics.

Is this distinction purely based on history and outcomes or is there something distinguishable in the brain? If the concepts of sexual selection and natural selection are considered, then it might be argued that the brain processes supporting an idea (i.e., a religion) that is capable of sustaining itself and growing through others are the most adaptive.

Such ideas probably require a balance between explaining the world and integrating with the world. What I mean by this is that religious ideas that survive likely have to have some generally successful characteristics. They must provide a clear and coherent mythology that can be transmitted from person to person and generation to generation. This requires the development not only of a well-developed mythology but of associated rituals as well. This mythology has to be internally consistent and must also relate to everyday beliefs and behaviors. In other words, the beliefs that are embodied in the myths and rituals must have a practical application in real life. A person must be able to survive and perform everyday survival activities such as finding food and having a secure place to live to raise a family, and hence, the next generation. Interestingly, most religions recognize the need for both the everyday person as well as the higher religious follower such as a monk or nun.

If everyone on Earth decided to become a monk or nun and live a life of celibacy, the human species, and religion itself, would die off pretty quickly. However, with the right amount and numbers, these hyper-religious individuals might provide both a societal as well as an individual goal to attain to. Perhaps they are somewhat like the "alpha male" or "queen bee," only instead of being essential for creating the next generation, they are essential for creating the belief system itself. The high ideals of religion are the target and are what maintain the larger religious framework.

Successful religious ideas also have to be changeable enough to be adaptive and be stable enough to maintain the basic elements of the religion. For example, Judaism had to modify its rules of the Sabbath to account for electricity and electrical devices. But keeping the Sabbath is still fundamental to what it means to be Jewish. Thus, for a religion to be successful, it needs to connect with large numbers of people and maintain a central set of beliefs, but allow for adaptability to occur over time to continue to be relevant. There is an important balance that occurs to make any given religion able to survive.

As an analogy, lots of people write lots of music, but some people are able to find the right words and melodies to touch the masses of people. The Beatles wrote songs such as "Let It Be" or "Hey Jude" that became enormously popular. For the millions of musicians out there who have written songs that no one has ever heard of, does that make them better or worse musicians than the Beatles? They all write music, but clearly there is something special about the brains of the Beatles for finding the right words and music that can resonate with millions of people. Religions operate in a similar manner, which ultimately is based on what the brain of the individual followers is doing. If the brain finds a good middle ground between beliefs and life, then the religion and the individuals are successful and continue. If the brain does not find a good middle ground, then they and their religion will likely fade away slowly over time, or suddenly in a severe action, such as in the case of a cult's mass suicide.

THE BELL CURVE OF HUMAN TRAITS

If a cult follower cannot engage in everyday life activities successfully, and if the cult's ideas are met with derision from a large group of others, then the brain of that person is likely unable to adaptively integrate the cult's beliefs. Ultimately, a person is able to integrate their religious and spiritual beliefs (even if they don't have them) to varying degrees of adaptability. From an evolutionary perspective, the main manner in which this happens is through a diversity of intensity levels or ability levels of the attribute. These diverse levels are typically distributed along a bell curve.[91]

The bell curve concept is particularly important in evolution. For any given characteristic, a bell curve distribution enables evolution to work. If everyone had the exact same characteristics, there would be no way to select for anyone. In other words, if all elk had the same size antlers and if all peacocks had the same colored plumage, females could not distinguish between them. Similarly, if all gazelles were the same speed, there would be no way to select for faster ones. So there needs to be some natural variability, but that variability has to revolve around some general characteristic. The majority of elk antlers are approximately 3 feet long, but some are substantially longer and some are substantially shorter. Those differences allow for mate selection of either larger or smaller antlers. But the bell curve itself is important for identifying the species itself. In other words, if elk didn't have antlers at all, they may not be identifiable as elk. Or if elk had huge antlers, they might be misidentified as moose. The point is that there is a central set of characteristics that ultimately define a given species and its general characteristics.

Extrapolating this thinking where human beings are concerned, there are many traits related to religion and sexuality that exist along a bell-type curve. For example, human beings have an overall average level of intelligence, but some are smarter, some are intellectually deficient, and occasionally some are Einsteins. This enables people to decide how intelligent a mate they want. Further, as one type of mate is selected—perhaps the more intelligent ones—the overall bell curve becomes shifted as individuals who are intellectually deficient end up not procreating. This shifting of the bell curve is also important in evolution as it can result in minor modifications of a species without changing it completely. Eventually, if human beings

---

91   Ridley M. *Evolution*. 3rd ed. Blackwell Publishing; 2004; O'Boyle E Jr, Aguinis H. The best and the rest: revisiting the norm of normality of individual performance. *Personnel Psychology*. 2012;65:79-119.

selected for highly intelligent mates with huge heads, we might evolve into the next species in the *Homo* lineage.

The same can be true for religion. There are some people for whom religion is easy to accept and follow and others who find it harder to engage. This creates a continuum that enables people to select individuals who express more or less religion and spirituality in their life. In this way, some groups might become more religious while others become less over time. These represent different types of belief systems about the world. The core beliefs are in the heart of the bell curve while those with intensely atheistic or hyper-religious views lie on the outer shoulders of the curve.

From a purely philosophical perspective, it might be challenging to determine which belief system along a continuum is "correct"—that is, atheist versus agnostic versus believer versus monk—but from a neurotheological perspective, one belief system may at least be shown to be more adaptive. Similarly, different traditions compare to others based on how "successful" they are in continuing from one generation to the next. If the ideas of a religious tradition provide a large number of people with the meaning in life they desire so that they follow the tradition and pass it on to their children, then the religion itself continues. But if religious ideas or traditions become unwieldy or irrelevant, people will stop following them, and as a belief system, the religion will ultimately die out. It is certainly a noteworthy fact that most of the major religions have survived far longer than any empire or political system. The monotheistic traditions are 1500 to several thousand years old and Buddhism and Hinduism are similarly several thousand years old.

Importantly, the adaptability of a religious tradition does not necessarily reflect its truth value, but rather how well it can be incorporated and maintained in people's lives. Thus, while epistemology, or the ascertaining of which belief system is closest to reality, is likely to be useful in establishing the adaptability of a belief system, it is not inherently required.

We will consider epistemological questions in the final chapter, but permit here one more point about sexual reproduction and adaptability. If an animal attempts sex with animals from lots of different species, it likely is not going to get them anywhere evolutionarily speaking. They are only going to produce offspring if they mate with their own species because sexual reproduction requires two animals that are genetically similar. On the other hand, a new species might arise from the mating of two similar species. This is the case where human evolution is concerned, since there is substantial evidence to show that *Homo sapiens* and Neanderthals mated. About 3% to 4% of human DNA is from Neanderthals.[92] And maybe some of the physical robustness of the Neanderthals helped human beings survive harsh environments more effectively.

Religious individuals and religions probably share similar aspects in terms of their development. If religions comingle beliefs through mating, they will slowly evolve but still maintain the primary tenets that make up their belief system. For example, as Christianity moved through the Middle Ages, it adopted pagan elements but not enough to modify its basic beliefs. However, if many cross interactions occur, the religion might transition into a completely new belief system. The Mormon faith acknowledges Jesus as the messiah but is so distinct from Christianity that it became its own new religion. Whether that new religion is more accurate, or simply easier for people to understand and believe, is something that remains to be evaluated both scientifically and spiritually.

CONNECTING HYPER-RELIGIOUSNESS AND HYPERSEXUALITY

What about the similarities and differences between hyper-religious and hypersexual individuals? Analogous to substance abuse, there are probably a number of overlapping neurochemical changes. The dopamine and opiate systems are likely involved in both since the feeling of ecstasy and bliss is a part of both sexual and spiritual experience. Both sexual and spiritual experiences become highly desired to be experienced again. Perhaps something that is unique to religious experience is that they are much less frequent and cannot be reliably produced. Sexual orgasm is something

---

92   Reilly PF, Tjahjadi A, Miller SL, Akey JM, Tucci S. The contribution of Neanderthal introgression to modern human traits. *Curr Biol.* 2022;32(18):R970-R983. doi:10.1016/j .cub.2022.08.027.

that can be reliably produced and can be done frequently. However, are intense religious experiences the ultimate expression of the brain apparatus that is involved with sexual experience? Or could it be something completely different?

The overlap between sexuality and spirituality has frequently led psychiatrists to explore the potential of spirituality to help people with sexual and substance abuse disorders. Some of the most well-known and successful programs for addiction recovery include Alcoholics Anonymous and Narcotics Anonymous, which have similar approaches to help people fight their addiction and which are both grounded in spiritual beliefs.[93] First and foremost is the invocation of a higher power that becomes the focus of the person's life and an object to which the addiction can be "transferred" in some respect. It is not clear whether the addiction to drugs or alcohol is literally transferred to religious beliefs. Some early research suggested this might be the case while other studies have argued against that proposition.[94] However, it must be acknowledged that spirituality can play an important role in helping many people overcome their addictions.

In the end, sexuality and spirituality share much in common when it comes to addictive types of behavior. People can become obsessed and pursue sexuality and spirituality to levels that are maladaptive. The primary difference appears to be the potential upside. While the use of various substances in small amounts is not likely to cause too much trouble, it is rarely beneficial. Maybe a glass of wine a few times a week confers some heart benefits, but the larger risks associated with the use of alcohol are likely to outweigh them. And the World Health Organization indicates that

93   Galanter M, White WL, Khalsa J, Hansen H. A scoping review of spirituality in relation to substance use disorders: psychological, biological, and cultural issues. *J Addict Dis.* 2023;1-9. doi:10.1080/10550887.2023.2174785; Kelly JF, Abry A, Ferri M, Humphreys K. Alcoholics Anonymous and 12-step facilitation treatments for alcohol use disorder: a distillation of a 2020 Cochrane review for clinicians and policy makers. *Alcohol and Alcoholism.* 2020;55(6):641-651. doi: 10.1093/alcalc/agaa050.

94   Larson DB, Swyers JP, McCullough ME, eds. *Scientific Research on Spirituality and Health: A Consensus Report.* National Institute for Healthcare Research; 1998.

any alcohol is potentially bad for your health.[95] The same is true of drugs and smoking. There are minimal benefits other than making a person feel good. The difference is that religion in most cases, from small to substantial amounts, can be beneficial to health and well-being (barring the negative side of religion that does happen but is problematic in any amount).[96] Religion is far more adaptive generally speaking than the use of any substance. Perhaps certain drugs such as psychedelics can be helpful, but religious and spiritual traditions seem to be the most likely to provide benefits for human well-being both in the short term and long term.

---

95 World Health Organization. No level of alcohol consumption is safe for our health. World Health Organization. 2023. Accessed March 18, 2023. https://www.who.int/europe/news/item/04-01-2023-no-level-of-alcohol-consumption-is-safe-for-our-health.

96 Miller L. *The Spiritual Child*. St. Martin's Press; 2015; Lucchetti G, Koenig HG, Lucchetti ALG. Spirituality, religiousness, and mental health: a review of the current scientific evidence. *World J Clin Cases*. 2021;9(26):7620-7631.

CHAPTER 9

PSYCHOLOGY, SEXUALITY, AND GOD

Religion is an illusion, and it derives its strength from its readiness to fit in with our instinctual wishful impulses.

—Sigmund Freud, *New Introductory Lectures on Psychoanalysis*

THE PSYCHOLOGY OF RELIGION

The last two chapters dealt with the important relationship between sexuality and the brain as it pertains to biological processes and neurotransmitters. But the notion of addictions, in particular, begins to encroach on the broader topic of psychology. And there is clearly a close relationship between psychology, the brain, and sex. What we will focus on here is not just the overall relationship between psychology, the brain, and sex, but how that relationship interacts with religion and spirituality. After all, a great deal has been made in the field of psychology about the underlying forces leading to religious and spiritual beliefs and behaviors. Unfortunately, much of psychology and psychiatry has looked at religion and spirituality in a more negative or even pathological way. This has prompted some to consider religiousness a kind of disorder, illusion, or delusion.[97]

In the Diagnostic and Statistical Manual of Mental Disorders (DSM), a comprehensive guidebook for mental health professionals, it does not provide a formal definition of religion, but it does provide guidelines for

---

97   Dawkins R. *The God Delusion*. Mariner Books; 2006.

diagnosing and treating mental health disorders related to religious or spiritual beliefs.[98] One of the most notable diagnoses related to religion is: *religious or spiritual problems*. This category includes several disorders, including religious or spiritual distress, religious or spiritual problems related to a mental disorder, and religious or spiritual problems related to a psychosocial stressor. These diagnoses are intended to capture situations in which an individual's religious or spiritual beliefs or practices are causing significant distress or impairment. As discussed in the previous chapter on addictions, one of the important points here is that spirituality and religion can be adaptive or maladaptive depending on how it personally affects someone and interferes with or enhances their life.

The DSM also includes a diagnosis for delusional disorder, which can sometimes be related to religious or spiritual beliefs. Individuals with delusional disorder may hold fixed, false beliefs that are not consistent with their culture or religious traditions. These delusions may take on religious or spiritual themes, such as believing that they have been chosen by God for a special mission or that they are possessed by demons.

Again, there can be a fine line between disorder and profound beliefs. A nun or monk might feel *called* or *chosen* to become deeply religious. This sense of a calling is commonly expressed among deeply religious individuals. But is a sense of calling an abnormality? Psychologically speaking, the sense of calling can border on the delusional. But since so many individuals with hyper-religious beliefs talk about experiencing such a feeling, perhaps this is a normal way in which religiousness is manifested. In fact, if you recall that the notion of surrender is a core element of enlightenment experiences, such a sense of surrendering or following God can be very much like a feeling of calling. Thus, we must be careful how much this notion is pathologized.

Does a sense of calling relate at all to sexuality and mating? Many people feel that they were called by their spouse or lover early in the process. People feel a sense of magic, mystery, or serendipity. On one hand, we might realistically recognize that there are many potential mates for

---

98   American Psychiatric Association. *Diagnostic and Statistical Manual of Mental Disorders.* 5th ed. American Psychiatric Association; 2013.

each of us. But when that ritualistic connection is made, we feel as if there is one and only one person for us. From a brain perspective, this makes sense as we have already described how rituals bring two individuals together. And current research shows that when we make an intimate connection with another person, our brain resonates with them—literally. Brain scan and electroencephalography (EEG) studies show that the electrical wave patterns of people in love or deeply connected to each other begin to appear the same.[99] The more profound the connection that is felt, the stronger the resonance. This likely utilizes the same social areas of the brain involved in practices like OM and in the mating behavior of humans and other animals. By feeling drawn or called to another person, we allow for a breaking down of the boundaries between ourselves and that other person. When elaborated in the human brain, it can be expanded to a feeling of religious calling in which the person feels deeply connected to the universe or God.

Despite having limitations with regard to how well it handles religion and spirituality, the DSM remains an important tool for mental health professionals who work with individuals who are struggling with religious or spiritual issues. By providing standardized criteria for diagnosis and treatment, the DSM can help ensure that individuals receive appropriate care that is tailored to their specific needs and experiences. While the DSM does not provide a comprehensive description of religion itself, it does recognize the significant impact that religious and spiritual beliefs can have on mental health and well-being. By taking a nuanced and culturally sensitive approach to these issues, mental health professionals can help individuals navigate the complex interplay between religion, spirituality, and mental health.

But where did the fields of psychology and psychiatry start out when it comes to religious and spiritual beliefs? It began with the initial work of William James, the noted psychologist and philosopher who presented his psychological ideas about religious experience in his Gifford Lecture

---

99   Kinreich S, Djalovski A, Kraus L, Louzoun Y, Feldman R. Brain-to-brain synchrony during naturalistic social interactions. *Sci Rep.* 2017;7(1):17060. doi:10.1038/s41598-017-17339-5.

presentation in 1902 entitled *The Varieties of Religious Experience.*[100] He recognized that there are both positive and negative influences of religion on the human psyche as he explored topics such as the sick soul, saintliness, and mystical experience. He laid out a description of religious experiences that provided a foundation for much future exploration, including the current work, in terms of how the mind intersects with religious and spiritual phenomena. James described these varieties but did not seek to explain their psychological or neurological workings in much detail. This had to wait for some of the most influential psychologists to rewrite the field—Sigmund Freud and Carl Jung.

FREUD, JUNG, AND THE RELIGIOUS PSYCHE

Although the psychology world has generally moved on from the incredible influence of Sigmund Freud's work in the early twentieth century, his overall impact on our approach to the mind and emotions is undeniable. It is also well known that part of his revolutionary approach was to base many of his ideas about psychology and psychological problems on sexuality. This ultimately has been looked upon with some scorn since it is difficult to relate every psychological problem to some sexually oriented issue, but perhaps it is worth relooking at this relationship in light of what we now know about the link between sexuality and spirituality.

Sigmund Freud is perhaps best known for his theories on the human psyche, particularly his ideas about the role of sexuality in human behavior. Freud believed that sexual energy was a fundamental aspect of human psychology and that it played a crucial role in shaping most of our personality and behavior.

One of Freud's most influential ideas was his concept of the "sexual drive," or libido. According to Freud, this innate sexual energy is present in all human beings from birth and drives human behavior, motivating people to seek out pleasure and satisfaction. Freud believed that the sexual libido was the primary motivator of human behavior and that it is expressed

---

100   James W. *The Varieties of Religious Experience.* Harvard University Press; 1902.

in a variety of ways, including sexual desires, fantasies, and activities. Given what we have been exploring throughout this book, it may be easier to see how this happens through the physiological processes that support sexuality and mating that ultimately became incorporated into virtually every aspect of the mind.

Sexually selective characteristics typically become most prominent in animals when they mature enough to begin mating. In a similar manner, Freud believed that human sexuality developed in stages, with each stage characterized by a different focus of the sexual energy.[101] Where the connection between sexuality and behavior might differ in Freud's work is how he implicated sex even in infants. In his theory of psychosexual development, Freud identified five stages: oral, anal, phallic, latent, and genital. Each stage was associated with different physical and psychological changes, and disruptions or fixations at any stage could lead to later psychological problems.

According to Freud, the oral stage is the first stage of psychosexual development, occurring from birth to around 18 months of age. During this stage, infants experience sexual pleasure through the mouth, primarily through breastfeeding or sucking on objects. While it probably goes too far to characterize such behaviors as overtly sexual, it does make sense that they would be pleasurable. As stated earlier, the brain evolved in order to experience sexual pleasure, but this was probably built on the more basic pleasure centers of the brain that are required for most primary life functions such as eating, sleeping, and of course, sex. These activities have to be pleasurable for an animal or else it won't engage them and won't survive. Freud believed that disruptions or fixations at this stage could lead to later problems such as overeating, smoking, or alcoholism. Whether such a connection is directly related between problems in this stage and psychological disorders is unclear, but most psychologists today do not agree that such a defined link exists.

The anal stage, which occurs from around 18 months to three years of

101   Freud S. Three essays on the theory of sexuality. In: Strachey J, ed. *The Standard Edition of the Complete Psychological Works of Sigmund Freud, Volume VII (1901-1905): A Case of Hysteria, Three Essays on Sexuality and Other Works.* Hogarth Press; 1953:123-246.

age, is characterized by pleasure derived from the control of bodily functions. Freud believed that during this stage, children experience pleasure from retaining and releasing feces, and that disruptions or fixations at this stage could lead to later psychological problems such as anal retentiveness or an anal-expulsive personality. It is certainly fascinating to consider how the focus on anal sensations might relate more broadly to sexuality. Anal sex is something that many people have engaged in. However, most religions condemn anal sex as an abnormal form of sexuality. This is particularly the case as it pertains to homosexuality that many orthodox religions similarly feel is abnormal. Thus, whether Freud got it right that people can sometimes be focused on the anal region as a form of sexuality that leads to other psychological disorders is uncertain. But it is interesting that anal sex can be pleasurable for both individuals involved. From an evolutionary perspective, some have postulated that anal sex enables larger males to dominate smaller males but also enables the smaller males to gain protection from those larger males by satisfying sexual urges. Others have suggested it is just curious human beings looking for new sensations. Whether this is an epiphenomenon or whether there is a true adaptive value for anal sex is unclear. But either way, anal sex, along with many other more unusual elements of sexuality, likely rely on similar biology.

The phallic stage, which occurs from around three to six years of age, is characterized by a focus on the genitals and the discovery of sexual differences between boys and girls. According to Freud, children experience sexual attraction to their opposite-sex parent and jealousy toward their same-sex parent during this stage, a phenomenon he called the Oedipus complex. This term derives from the classic Greek myth of the King Oedipus who ends up killing his father and marrying his mother, even though this is not what he intended to do. Freud believed that the resolution of this complex was crucial for healthy adult sexuality. One of the particularly problematic aspects of the phallic stage idea is that it is based primarily on male development. Freud does differentiate what happens during this phase with males becoming obsessed with their own penis and females becoming fixated on the fact that they do not have a penis—the well-known concept of "penis envy."

The latent stage, which occurs from around six years to puberty, is a period of relative sexual calm, during which children's sexual energy is focused on nonsexual activities such as play and learning. Finally, the genital stage, which begins at puberty and continues through adulthood, is characterized by a renewed focus on the genitals and sexual relationships with others. In the context of sexual selection, such a profound interest in the genitals occurring during puberty makes sense since this is when a person develops the ability to actually mate and have children.

Freud's views on sexuality have been the subject of much debate and criticism over the years. Some have criticized his theories as overly simplistic or reductionistic, while others have argued that they are fundamentally flawed, depending too much on sexuality and an inaccurate analysis of human development. Nevertheless, Freud's ideas continue to be influential in modern psychology and continue to inspire new research in the field. For example, recent research has explored the ways in which early experiences of sexual abuse or trauma can impact the development of the libido and lead to later psychological problems. Other researchers have explored the role of cultural and social factors in shaping sexual desire and behavior, and how these factors interact with biological and psychological processes.

Relevant to this book, Freud took the discussion about sexuality and the mind a step further by proposing a unique perspective on the relationship between sexuality and religion. He believed religion played a significant role in controlling and sublimating sexual desires, particularly those associated with the Oedipus complex.[102] Religion, in his view, served to repress these desires by imposing strict moral codes and norms on sexual behavior.

Freud argued that religious beliefs and practices allowed individuals to express their deepest desires and anxieties in symbolic form. For example,

---

102   Freud S. Obsessive actions and religious practices. In: Strachey J, ed. *The Standard Edition of the Complete Psychological Works of Sigmund Freud, Volume IX (1906-1908): Jensen's 'Gradiva' and Other Works.* Hogarth Press; 1953:115-128; Freud S. Totem and taboo. In: Strachey J, ed. *The Standard Edition of the Complete Psychological Works of Sigmund Freud, Volume XIII (1913-1914): Totem and Taboo and Other Works.* Hogarth Press; 1953.

he suggested that religious rituals, such as confession and penance, were a way for individuals to symbolically purify themselves of their sexual desires and impulses. Furthermore, Freud believed that religious symbols and myths reflected deep-seated sexual fantasies and desires. He suggested that the Christian concept of the Trinity represented a symbolic representation of the Oedipus complex, with the Father representing the same-sex parent, the Son representing the child, and the Holy Spirit representing the opposite-sex parent. While Freud's theories on the relationship between religion and sexuality have likewise been subject to criticism and debate, our research into the brain during sexual and spiritual practices might open new doors for a better understanding of this relationship.

Carl Jung, a renowned Swiss psychologist, had a unique perspective on sexuality that was heavily influenced by his work in analytical psychology. In Jung's view, sexuality was not simply a biological or instinctual drive, but rather an essential aspect of the human psyche that was intimately connected to the process of individuation. According to Jung, individuation was the process by which people strive toward wholeness and completeness, seeking to integrate all aspects of their psyche, including the unconscious. Sexuality, in his view, was a key aspect of this process, serving as a powerful force that could drive individuals toward self-discovery and personal growth.

Jung also believed that sexuality was closely linked to archetypes, universal patterns of symbols and imagery that were shared by all human beings.[103] He argued that sexual desires and fantasies could serve as a means of accessing and exploring these archetypes, providing individuals with insights into their own psyche and the larger collective unconscious.

One of Jung's most significant contributions to the study of sexuality was his theory of *anima* and *animus*. According to Jung, *anima* represents the feminine aspect of the male psyche, while *animus* represents the masculine aspect of the female psyche. He believed that the integration of these archetypes was essential for achieving psychological balance and wholeness. This sounds quite similar to various religious interpretations of how males and females came about and interact with each other.

---

103   Jung CG. *The Archetypes and the Collective Unconscious*. Bollingen; 1969.

Jung also explored the ways in which sexuality could be expressed through artistic and creative endeavors. He argued that artistic expression provided individuals with a means of accessing their deepest desires and emotions, allowing them to express and explore their sexuality in a safe and socially acceptable manner.

Carl Jung, like Freud before him, had a unique perspective on the relationship between sexuality and religion.[104] Jung believed that as a fundamental aspect of the human psyche, sexuality was closely connected to religious experience and expression. One of Jung's most significant contributions to the study of sexuality and religion was his theory of the transcendent function. According to Jung, the transcendent function was a psychological process that involved the integration of conscious and unconscious aspects of the psyche, leading to a state of greater wholeness and integration. He believed that sexuality and religious experience were both powerful forces that could facilitate this process of integration, allowing individuals to access deeper aspects of their psyche and the collective unconscious.

Jung also explored ways in which religious symbolism and mythology were intimately connected to sexual imagery and desire. He argued that religious myths and symbols often represented universal archetypes that were deeply rooted in the human psyche, including archetypes related to sexuality and expression of sexual desire. As we considered earlier, it looks like there is a deep connection between the myths that arise around sexuality, mating, and fertility, with those that arise around religious and spiritual belief systems.

For example, Jung suggested that the Christian concept of the Holy Trinity was a symbolic representation of the union between the masculine and feminine aspects of the psyche. Thus, in the trinity, Jung also saw a representation of the human psyche as males have an unconscious feminine anima and females have an unconscious masculine animus. These two sides exist and come together to form the self in each person. He believed that this union was necessary for achieving psychological balance and wholeness and that it was often expressed through religious and spiritual experiences.

---

104   Jung CG. *Psychology and Religion: West and East*. Routledge; 1977.

Jung also believed that sexual experience and expression could serve as a means of accessing the divine or transcendent realm.[105] He argued that sexual ecstasy and the experience of orgasm were similar to religious experiences of transcendence, in that they involved a dissolution of the ego and a sense of merging with a larger, more universal reality. It is interesting that we see such a conclusion from Jung almost 100 years before we have the brain scan studies of OM to show how that relationship occurs. Our research shows how sexuality and spirituality affect the same brain pathways, particularly involving the parietal and frontal lobe, that lead to feelings of transcendence and ecstasy.

HOW SPIRITUALITY AND RELIGION CAN BE THERAPEUTIC

Given this psychological background regarding sexuality, spirituality, and psychology, it is worth reflecting more deeply on how religious and spiritual concepts can be used within the therapeutic setting in psychology. As we have seen, religion and spirituality have long been recognized as important factors in mental health and well-being. In fact, the famous German psychologist and philosopher, Erich Fromm frequently described how healthy sexuality could be an important expression of a person's spirituality. Further, he indicated that authentic sexual experiences could be part of a broader spiritual or humanistic perspective, especially if they were based in love, mutual respect, and emotional intimacy.[106] Fromm's work is in many ways a psychological prelude to some of the arguments made in this book—that there is a strong interconnectedness between sexuality and religion. We are now able to add in the perspective of neuroscience that not only helps us understand this relationship but shows how integral spirituality is in the elaboration of religious and spiritual phenomena.

By affecting specific neurotransmitters along with brain areas that

---

105   Jung CG. *The Undiscovered Self.* Signet; 1957.

106   Fromm E. *Love, Sexuality, and Matriarchy: About Gender.* Funk R, ed. Fromm Intl; 1997.

regulate emotions and foster self-transcendence, religious and spiritual practices have the potential to be beneficial in psychology. For example, religion and spirituality are frequently cited as a primary source of coping for people facing various life stressors such as the diagnosis of a physical problem such as cancer, significant mental disorders such as depression, or loss of a loved one.[107] For such reasons, many mental health professionals have begun to incorporate religious and spiritual practices into their psychotherapeutic approaches.[108]

One way in which religion can be incorporated into psychotherapy is through the use of prayer or meditation. We have already considered the results of our meditation studies that show changes in the brain during practices like prayer, meditation, or OM. The studies I have been involved with have also revealed another effect of these practices on the brain over long periods of time. Even when a person is not performing a spiritual practice, by doing practices over and over, and for many years, the brain literally changes. This has important implications for modifying the brain in people dealing with various mental health problems or who simply want to keep their brain as healthy as possible.

The analogy I like to use is to think of the brain as a muscle. When you lift weights, a muscle becomes thicker and stronger. The brain reacts similarly, with prayer and meditation working as the stimulus. Studies have shown that long-term meditators, those practicing for many years, have thicker frontal lobes than nonmeditators.[109] Longitudinal studies from my research group have shown that if you start a meditation practice today, after only eight weeks, the frontal lobes are more active at rest, and this

107 Pargament KI. *The Psychology of Religion and Coping: Theory, Research, Practice*. Guilford Press; 1997.

108 Hook JN, Worthington EL Jr, Davis DE, Jennings DJ 2nd, Gartner AL, Hook JP. Empirically supported religious and spiritual therapies. *J Clin Psychol*. 2010;66(1):46-72; Rosmarin DH, Pargament KI, Flannelly KJ. Incorporating clients' religious and spiritual beliefs in psychotherapy: introduction to the special section. *J Clin Psychol*. 2009;65(2):131-134. https://doi.org/10.

109 Lazar SW, Kerr CE, Wasserman RH, et al. Meditation experience is associated with increased cortical thickness. *Neuroreport*. 2005;16(17):1893-1897.

increase is correlated with improvements in concentration and memory along with reductions in anxiety and depression symptoms. This all makes sense since the frontal lobes are involved in concentration and also the regulation of emotions.

In our OM study, we similarly showed long-term changes in the brain's function. In long-term OM practitioners, there was significantly lower metabolism in several areas of the frontal, temporal, and parietal lobes, as well as the anterior cingulate, insula, and thalamus, compared to nonmeditating controls. These changes were observed in both males and females but were more prominent in the females. While decreased metabolism might seem counter to the muscle analogy, a different way of interpreting such a change in the brain is that these areas have become more efficient or more receptive. The implication is that by doing the OM practice, people alter the function in their brain, particularly in emotional and social areas. Hence, they may be more receptive and open to the emotions and social connections with others.

Virtually all types of spiritual practices can have a long-term effect on the brain and on the person. The exact effect may depend on what the practice actually strives to do—making a social connection, reducing stress, feeling joy, etc. Many religious traditions place a strong emphasis on prayer or meditation as a means of connecting with a higher power or finding inner peace. In psychotherapy, prayer and meditation can be used to help clients manage stress and anxiety, increase their sense of well-being, and develop a deeper sense of meaning and purpose in life.

Another way in which religion can be incorporated into psychotherapy is through the use of religious rituals and practices. Many religious traditions have specific rituals or practices that are designed to promote healing and well-being. For example, the Catholic Church offers the sacrament of reconciliation, which is designed to help individuals find forgiveness and peace through confession and absolution. Similarly, some Native American tribes use sweat lodges as a way of purifying the body and mind. Each of these approaches has the potential to be beneficial in the right setting for the right individuals.

Religious beliefs and practices can also be used as a source of strength and support in psychotherapy. Many individuals draw on their faith as a source of comfort and guidance during times of stress or crisis.[110] In therapy, mental health professionals can help clients identify and explore the ways in which their religious beliefs and practices can be a source of strength and resilience.

However, there are also challenges associated with incorporating religion into psychotherapy. For example, clients may hold beliefs that are different from those of their therapist, which can create tension or conflict. Additionally, some individuals may have had negative experiences with religion or may feel uncomfortable discussing their beliefs in a therapy setting, especially if the therapist holds different religious or spiritual views.

Despite these challenges, research has shown that incorporating religion into psychotherapy can be beneficial for many individuals. For example, a study published in the *Journal of Consulting and Clinical Psychology* found that individuals who received religiously integrated psychotherapy experienced greater improvements in depressive symptoms than those who received nonreligious psychotherapy.[111]

It remains to be seen how valuable integrating religious and spiritual concepts into traditional psychotherapeutic interventions might be to improve mental health problems. It might be more useful in people who already hold strong religious or spiritual beliefs, although more secular practices such as meditation or yoga might be useful in many people, including those without religious beliefs. The relationship between psychology, the brain, spirituality, and sexuality is really only beginning to be elucidated. Having more and more research that observes the clinical as

110 López-Sierra HE, Rodríguez-Sánchez J. The supportive roles of religion and spirituality in end-of-life and palliative care of patients with cancer in a culturally diverse context: a literature review. *Curr Opin Support Palliat Care.* 2015;9(1):87-95; de Diego-Cordero R, Ávila-Mantilla A, Vega-Escaño J, Lucchetti G, Badanta B. The role of spirituality and religiosity in healthcare during the COVID-19 pandemic: an integrative review of the scientific literature. *J Relig Health.* 2022;61(3):2168-2197.

111 Propst LR, Ostrom R, Watkins P, Dean T, Mashburn D. Comparative efficacy of religious and nonreligious cognitive-behavior therapy for the treatment of clinical depression in religious individuals. *J Consult Clin Psychol.* 1992;60:94-103.

well as the biological impact of religion on the human psyche will be essential for helping us find the most effective ways of supporting mental health and well-being for everyone.

CHAPTER 10

THE DARK SIDE OF SEXUALITY AND RELIGION

Luke: "Is the Dark Side stronger?"
Yoda: "No. Quicker, easier, more seductive."
—Star Wars: Episode V—The Empire Strikes Back

Obi Wan Kenobi: "Vader was seduced by the dark side of the Force."
—Star Wars: Episode IV—A New Hope

SEDUCTION AND THE DARK SIDE

Whenever we talk about evil, much like in the highly popular *Star Wars* movies, we often use the term "seduction." The word seduction stems from Latin and literally means "leading astray." It theoretically can have a positive or negative connotation, but usually it refers to the negative.

Seduction has always played a prominent role in both sexuality and spirituality. Sexually, it might be fun to seduce your spouse, providing a little intrigue and fantasy into sexual activity. But seducing someone who you should not be having sex with can be very problematic, and sometimes even illegal. Similarly, religion has often been associated with promoting mental well-being along with moral and ethical behavior, including in the realm of sexuality. However, there have been many instances in which religious individuals or organizations have engaged in inappropriate beliefs and behaviors. Some religious traditions have ended up supporting pedophilia or other terrible sexual practices, and sometimes they have vilified people who engage in sexual practices deemed inappropriate by that tradition.

It seems, then, that there is a potential dark side to both spirituality and sexuality. And perhaps the seductive process in both circumstances relies on the same underlying physiology plunging both down dark paths toward immorality and evil.

SEXUAL ABUSE FROM THE OFFENDER PERSPECTIVE

Exploring the neuropsychology of sexual offenders can shed light on the underlying cognitive and neurological factors of their behavior. And hopefully, in the end, understanding these mechanisms can inform prevention strategies, intervention programs, and treatment approaches.

To begin with, there are many studies that have tried to get at the neurological underpinnings of abnormal and abusive sexual behavior. Not surprisingly, it involves many areas of the brain that control behaviors, emotions, and sexual feelings. One way to think about sexual abusers is that they either have poor control mechanisms or have emotions and sexual feelings that are so strong that even normal control mechanisms strain against them. In this latter case, they can't control their hypersexual feelings.

Offenders of sexual abuse often exhibit deficits in executive functions, including impulse control, decision-making, and inhibition, that are localized to the frontal lobes.[112] In fact, brain imaging studies have shown reduced activation and structural abnormalities in the frontal regions of the brain, particularly the prefrontal cortex, in individuals who commit sexual offenses.[113] Thus, the frontal lobes that normally help to control our behaviors are not able to control them well in sexual offenders. The frontal lobes along with the temporal lobes are also involved in the processing of

---

112   Joyal CC, Black DN, Dassylva B. The neuropsychology and neurology of sexual deviance: a review and pilot study. *Sex Abuse*. 2007;19(2):155-73; Kneer J, Borchardt V, Kärgel C, et al. Diminished fronto-limbic functional connectivity in child sexual offenders. *J Psychiatr Res*. 2019;108:48-56.

113   Szczypiński J, Wypych M, Krasowska A, et al. Abnormal behavioral and neural responses in the right dorsolateral prefrontal cortex during emotional interference for cognitive control in pedophilic sex offenders. *J Psychiatr Res*. 2022;151:131-135.

social cues, sexual behavior regulation, and decision-making. These areas may also help a person understand how a potential sexual partner might be feeling, both positively and negatively.

Let's explore hypersexuality a bit more. Hypersexuality refers to an excessive or compulsive preoccupation with sexual thoughts, fantasies, or behaviors. While hypersexuality can manifest in various ways, it is crucial to distinguish between consensual, healthy sexual expression and problematic, harmful behaviors associated with sexual abuse. After all, if two hypersexual people engage in lots of sex, there really is no problem with that, at least according to the couple. But if a hypersexual person becomes overly aggressive and misinterprets another person's feelings, sexual abuse or rape can occur. In the first place, human beings in general are highly sexual and so the potential for sexual abuse does not always require pathological levels of sexuality. But understanding the extremes can help us understand how and why sexual abuse seems so prevalent, perhaps as high as affecting 20% of the population.

There are a number of brain areas involved in hypersexuality. To begin, the limbic system, which includes structures such as the amygdala and the hippocampus, are frequently associated with intense emotions and sexuality. Dysfunction in the limbic system has been associated with increased sexual motivation, heightened reward sensitivity, and the reinforcement of hypersexual behaviors.[114] Dysregulation in the anterior cingulate cortex that balances the frontal lobes and the limbic areas may impact impulse control and contribute to the pursuit of immediate sexual gratification in individuals with hypersexuality.[115]

---

114 Voon V, Mole TB, Banca P, et al. Neural correlates of sexual cue reactivity in individuals with and without compulsive sexual behaviours. *PLoS One.* 2014;9(7):e102419. doi: 10.1371/journal.pone.0102419; Kühn S, Gallinat J. Neurobiological basis of hypersexuality. *Int Rev Neurobiol.* 2016;129:67-83. doi: 10.1016/bs.irn.2016.04.002.

115 Hammes J, Theis H, Giehl K, et al. Dopamine metabolism of the nucleus accumbens and fronto-striatal connectivity modulate impulse control. *Brain.* 2019;142(3):733-743; Mata-Marín D, Pineda-Pardo JÁ, Michiels M, et al. A circuit-based approach to modulate hypersexuality in Parkinson's disease. *Psychiatry Clin Neurosci.* 2023;77(4):223-232. doi: 10.1111/pcn.13523.

The dopamine areas of the brain are involved with reward processing and the experience of pleasure. Abnormalities in the dopamine areas of the brain have been linked to heightened sexual desire, compulsive sexual behaviors, and the reinforcement of hypersexual behaviors.[116]

Our old friend the hypothalamus plays a central role in regulating sexual behavior and physiological responses associated with sexual arousal.[117] You may recall from our earlier discussion that the hypothalamus regulates hormones, so the estrogen and testosterone that make us feel sexy come from this brain structure. In addition, the hypothalamus regulates our autonomic nervous system, which is essential for sexual function and orgasm.

There is another side to hypersexuality which is that engaging in hypersexual behaviors may provide temporary relief or distraction from psychological pain, albeit at the expense of others. Thus, for certain sexual abusers, hypersexuality may serve as a maladaptive coping mechanism to manage underlying emotional distress, such as prior emotional traumas, anxiety, or low self-esteem. This also can lead sexual abusers to develop various types of cognitive distortions, such as rationalizations and justifications, which enable the individual to minimize in their own mind the harm caused by their actions. Such cognitive distortions were likely prominent in well-known cases such as with the Catholic Church. After all, how could priests sexually abuse children from a moral or religious perspective? Clearly their brain was engaged in some cognitive gymnastics to find a way to justify their inappropriately lustful actions. These cognitive distortions may contribute to a self-perpetuating cycle of hypersexual behaviors and the perpetration of sexual abuse.

While we can point to some of these brain processes—emotional, cognitive, and sexual—there is another line of evidence that helps us understand such behaviors. This has to do with the environmental influences on

---

116 Mata-Marín D, Pineda-Pardo JÁ, Michiels M, et al. A circuit-based approach to modulate hypersexuality in Parkinson's disease. *Psychiatry Clin Neurosci.* 2023;77(4):223-232. doi: 10.1111/pcn.13523

117 Poeppl TB, Langguth B, Rupprecht R, et al. The neural basis of sex differences in sexual behavior: a quantitative meta-analysis. *Front Neuroendocrinol.* 2016;43:28-43. doi: 10.1016/j.yfrne.2016.10.001.

sexual abusers. The world is a very toxic place with all sorts of hormones, antibiotics, and toxic substances being used in various industries, including the food and building industry. We are constantly exposed to these toxic substances in the foods we eat, the water we drink, and in the buildings we live in. Neurochemical imbalances, hormonal dysregulation, and brain abnormalities from exposure to various hormones and toxins in the environment have been shown to affect the brain and might contribute to bizarre sexual behaviors.[118]

A history of psychological traumas also appear to play a prominent role in shaping the brain of sexual abusers. Such traumas affect the frontal lobes from developing properly along with the amygdala and hypothalamus, all of which may contribute to heightened sexual drive and difficulty controlling impulses. Early exposure to pornography, early sexualization, and a history of childhood sexual abuse can also play a role.[119] Adverse childhood experiences such as childhood trauma, neglect, and abuse are prevalent among offenders of sexual abuse.[120] Such experiences have likewise been associated with abnormal brain function in the same areas we have been discussing. Thus, the impact of adverse childhood experiences on brain development and the subsequent emergence of maladaptive cognitive and emotional patterns can contribute to the development of offending behaviors.

SEXUAL ABUSE FROM THE VICTIM PERSPECTIVE

Sexual abuse is a profoundly distressing experience that can have long-lasting psychological and neurological consequences for survivors. Neurologically, sexual abuse triggers a significant stress response in the brain and

---

118 Kruger THC, Sinke C, Kneer J, et al. Child sexual offenders show prenatal and epigenetic alterations of the androgen system. *Transl Psychiatry*. 2019;9(1):28. doi: 10.1038/ s41398-018-0326-0.

119 Simons DA, Wurtele SK, Durham RL. Developmental experiences of child sexual abusers and rapists. *Child Abuse Negl*. 2008;32(5):549-60.

120 Levenson JS, Willis GM, Prescott DS. Adverse childhood experiences in the lives of male sex offenders: implications for trauma-informed care. *Sex Abuse*. 2016;28(4):340-59.

body. The hypothalamic-pituitary-adrenal axis (sometimes called the HPA axis), which regulates the stress response, becomes dysregulated in response to trauma. Studies have found alterations in cortisol levels that are increased by the hypothalamus functioning in individuals who have experienced sexual abuse, indicating long-term changes in stress regulation.[121] It is interesting that the hypothalamus that regulates positive sexual activity and sexual pleasure also is activated when it turns negative and distressing.

Sexual abuse can also impact brain structures involved in emotional processing, such as the amygdala, hippocampus, and prefrontal cortex. These regions play a critical role in memory, emotion regulation, and fear processing. Neuroimaging studies have demonstrated structural and functional changes in the brains of individuals who have experienced sexual abuse, including alterations in gray matter volume and how different parts of the brain connect with each other.[122]

These negative physiological effects underlie the longer-term response of sexual abuse survivors typically leading to symptoms of PTSD, including intrusive memories, hyperarousal, avoidance, and negative alterations in cognition and mood. Research has linked PTSD symptoms to alterations in brain regions involved in fear conditioning and emotion regulation, such as the amygdala and prefrontal cortex.[123]

Sometimes, if the abuse is severe enough, the person can experience dissociation which represents a disconnection from one's thoughts, emotions,

121   Shenk CE, Felt JM, Ram N, et al. Cortisol trajectories measured prospectively across thirty years of female development following exposure to childhood sexual abuse: moderation by epigenetic age acceleration at midlife. *Psychoneuroendocrinology.* 2022;136:105606. doi: 10.1016/j.psyneuen.2021.105606.

122   Korgaonkar MS, Breukelaar IA, Felmingham K, Williams LM, Bryant RA. Association of neural connectome with early experiences of abuse in adults. *JAMA Netw Open.* 2023;6(1):e2253082. doi: 10.1001/jamanetworkopen.2022.53082.

123   Alexandra Kredlow M, Fenster RJ, Laurent ES, Ressler KJ, Phelps EA. Prefrontal cortex, amygdala, and threat processing: implications for PTSD. *Neuropsychopharmacology.* 2022;47(1):247-259. doi: 10.1038/s41386-021-01155-7; Landré L, Destrieux C, Andersson F, et al. Working memory processing of traumatic material in women with posttraumatic stress disorder. *J Psychiatry Neurosci.* 2012;37(2):87-94.

or memories as a means of psychological defense. Neuroimaging studies suggest that dissociation may involve disruptions in the connectivity between brain regions responsible for self-awareness, attention, and emotional processing.[124] And in response, sexual abuse can cause decreases in attention, concentration, and executive functions. Memory processes may also be affected, with survivors experiencing difficulties in memory retrieval or intrusive memories related to the abuse. Neuroimaging studies have revealed alterations in brain regions associated with memory, such as the hippocampus, in individuals who have experienced sexual abuse.

Fortunately, the brain's capacity to change in both negative and positive ways, often referred to as neuroplasticity, offers hope for recovery and healing. With appropriate interventions and support, survivors can build new neural connections and restore cognitive and emotional functioning to healthier levels. Psychotherapeutic approaches, such as trauma-focused therapy and cognitive-behavioral therapy, have shown effectiveness in promoting recovery and reducing PTSD symptoms.

Social support plays a crucial role in the recovery process. Positive social interactions and relationships contribute to resilience and buffer against the negative effects of sexual trauma. Research suggests that social support, as well as spiritual support, can influence neural mechanisms involved in emotion regulation, stress response, and overall well-being.

RELIGIOUS ABUSE FROM THE OFFENDER PERSPECTIVE

While many religions promote peace, compassion, and moral values, there have been many instances where religious institutions and individuals have been responsible for perpetrating abuses. It may be possible to explore how religious abuses parallel sexual abuses by examining the underlying factors that contribute to both types of behaviors, including power dynamics,

---

124   Blanco L, Nydegger LA, Camarillo G, Trinidad DR, Schramm E, Ames SL. Neurological changes in brain structure and functions among individuals with a history of childhood sexual abuse: a review. *Neurosci Biobehav Rev.* 2015;57:63-9.

ideological extremism, and the personal or sexual violations of other people. Some may point out that a distinction between religious and sexual abuse is that religious abuses typically occur at the group rather than the individual level. However, in the end, all abuses occur on the individual level. The individual perpetrators inflict that abuse on other individuals.

Historically, there have been many examples of abuse related to religious beliefs. One particularly well-known example of religious abuses was the Spanish Inquisition. The Inquisition targeted religious minorities, resulting in torture, forced conversions, and executions.[125] Even the witch hunts during the early modern period in Europe and America were fueled by religious beliefs and fears of satanic influence. Thousands of people, mainly women, were accused, tortured, and executed as witches.[126] Historical instances of colonization witnessed forced religious conversions and suppression of indigenous beliefs. European powers imposed their religious ideologies on native populations, often leading to cultural erasure.[127]

In recent times, religious extremism has been associated with acts of terrorism and violence. Extremist groups have exploited religious ideologies to justify their actions and target individuals and communities.[128] Certain religious cults have engaged in psychological manipulation, coercion, and abuse of their followers. Manipulative tactics employed by cult leaders can exploit vulnerable individuals and result in long-lasting harm.[129]

RELIGIOUS EXTREMISM

It seems that a common thread in all of these examples of religious abuse is that they are associated with extreme religious beliefs. One might even

125   Kamen H. *The Spanish Inquisition: A Historical Revision*. Yale University Press; 2014.

126   Levack BP. *The Witch-Hunt in Early Modern Europe*. Routledge; 2015.

127   Colley L. *Captives: Britain, Empire, and the World, 1600-1850*. Anchor Books; 2004.

128   Juergensmeyer M. *Terror in the Mind of God: The Global Rise of Religious Violence*. University of California Press; 2017.

129   Singer MT, Lalich J. *Cults in Our Midst: The Hidden Menace in Our Everyday Lives*. Jossey-Bass; 1995.

call the perpetrators of religious abuse *religious extremists*. However, as with sexual abuse, the human tendency toward strong religious beliefs does not require extreme beliefs to perpetrate abuse. The phenomenon of religious extremism is useful to explore, though, as it has implications for understanding all types of religious abuse. But how similar is the concept of religious extremism to hypersexuality? Perhaps they are closely linked like many other aspects of our earlier discussions relating sexuality to spirituality.

Understanding the underlying neuropsychological factors of the mindset of religious extremists is crucial for comprehending their beliefs, motivations, and behaviors. By unraveling these factors, we can gain valuable insights into the psychological mechanisms that contribute to the development and persistence of extremism, and subsequently, religious abuse.

Research suggests that religious extremists often exhibit reduced cognitive flexibility and a high degree of dogmatism. These individuals tend to adhere rigidly to their beliefs, resist contradictory information, and display "black-and-white" thinking. However, it is important to emphasize that this is not the same thing as intelligence. Many people have tried to link strong religious beliefs with a lack of intelligence, but it is far more likely that it is related to rigidity of beliefs and an unwillingness to explore and appreciate alternative belief systems.

In a similar manner, religious extremists may demonstrate something called *confirmation bias*, selectively seeking and interpreting information that supports their preexisting beliefs. I have previously described such biases in an earlier book, *Why We Believe What We Believe*.[130] This confirmation bias reinforces their extremist worldview and reinforces the cognitive and emotional aspects of their identity.

From a neurological perspective, we might understand this in the following way. As you create your own belief system, there are certain ideas that become stronger and stronger in your mind, and hence, in the neuronal connections in your brain. To break and reestablish these connections requires energy which challenges the brain to go through this process. More

---

130   Newberg AB, Waldman MR. *Why We Believe What We Believe: Uncovering Our Biological Need for Meaning, Spirituality, and Truth*. Free Press; 2006.

importantly, everyone ends up with belief systems that work for them and help them survive. Thus, confronting the possibility that there are alternative beliefs that might be better suited to your way of thinking leaves you feeling anxious. If you don't understand the world accurately, your survival is in jeopardy! Thus, between the need for a lot of neuronal energy to make new connections and the fear of being wrong, it is much easier to stick with your prevailing belief system.

Some people do this to the extreme, rejecting any new ideas or data, and becoming fervently and irrepressibly locked into a particular belief system. It takes over their thoughts, feelings, and behaviors. While this can happen on the individual level, how might religious groups and leaders take advantage of these neurological and psychological processes to amplify religious extremism?

Religious extremist groups often employ persuasive tactics that exploit emotional arousal to recruit and maintain members. The use of emotionally charged narratives that trigger emotional centers like the amygdala, and the manipulation of social identity, can facilitate the formation of a strong group affiliation. The fusion of personal identity with a religious extremist group can strengthen moral foundations, making individuals more willing to engage in extreme actions in the name of their cause.

The socialization process within religious extremist groups, including indoctrination and group reinforcement, shapes an individual's worldview and behavior. Social support, peer pressure, and a sense of belonging within the group contribute to the persistence of extremist beliefs.

Psychological vulnerabilities, such as a need for significance, feelings of marginalization, or personal crises, can make individuals more susceptible to radicalization. These individuals have emotional centers and frontal lobes that are particularly prone to be influenced and driven to extreme beliefs. Environmental factors, such as political instability, social injustice, or perceived threats to religious identity, can further fuel extremist ideologies.

The concept of brainwashing, also known as coercive persuasion or thought reform, is an approach that also shares many similarities with the kinds of religious indoctrination processes mentioned above. Coercive influence techniques exploit cognitive dissonance, psychological discomfort when beliefs and behaviors are inconsistent, by creating a discrepancy between an individual's existing beliefs and the desired belief system.

Brainwashing often relies on social influence principles, such as conformity and obedience to authority.[131] Compliance with group norms and pressure from charismatic leaders can lead individuals to adopt new beliefs and conform to the desired group ideology. Brainwashing techniques frequently involve controlling access to information and manipulating an individuals' perceptions of reality. By limiting exposure to dissenting opinions and providing biased information, manipulators can shape and distort individuals' understanding of the world.[132] As we discussed above, this process leads to stronger and stronger neuronal connections that support these beliefs—neurons that fire together wire together.

Emotional manipulation plays a crucial role in brainwashing, as strong emotions can override rational thinking. Fear induction, through threats, isolation, or punishment, creates emotional distress and makes individuals more susceptible to manipulation. Amazingly, research has shown that almost anyone can be subjected to such manipulation. Even good people can be converted into people who do very bad things to others, sometimes simply by asking them to do this. Studies like the Stanford Prison Experiment showed that when ordinary people were randomized to being either prisoners or guards, the situation quickly deteriorated into highly abusive behaviors.[133]

Brainwashing often aims to reconstruct an individual's identity and create a sense of dependency on the manipulator or group. This process involves severing ties with previous affiliations and gradually replacing them with a new group identity.[134]

Brainwashing techniques can have a profound impact on neural

---

131 Asch SE. Effects of group pressure upon the modification and distortion of judgments. In: Guetzkow H, ed. *Groups, Leadership and Men: Research in Human Relations*. Carnegie Press; 1951:177-190.

132 Lifton RJ. *Thought Reform and the Psychology of Totalism*. University of North Carolina Press; 1989.

133 Zimbardo PG. *The Lucifer Effect: Understanding How Good People Turn Evil*. Random House; 2007.

134 Singer MT, Lalich J. *Cults in Our Midst: The Hidden Menace in Our Everyday Lives*. Jossey-Bass; 1995.

pathways and brain functioning. For example, functional MRI studies have shown alterations in brain activity and connectivity associated with coercive influence, including changes in the prefrontal cortex, amygdala, and hippocampus. Such changes contribute to increased suggestibility, decreased critical thinking, and heightened emotional responses.[135] In this way, we can see similarities in the underlying brain areas that affect brainwashing, religion, and sexuality. While these activities can overtake the brain, the hope is that it is done for good purposes rather than bad ones.

SPECIFIC EXAMPLES OF SEXUAL ABUSE ASSOCIATED WITH RELIGIOUS OR SPIRITUAL GROUPS

While religious and spiritual abuses have occurred throughout history, there are several more modern ones that are worth looking at to better understand how and why they occur. These religious abuses are particularly notable as they overlap with sexual abuse. It is important to state up front that most abuses of this kind do not represent the entirety of a given group, and certainly not all of its members. Further, just because several group leaders or individuals perpetrate abuse on others, this does not mean that the religion itself or its ideals are inherently flawed or abusive in and of themselves. Of course, there are examples of specific cults in which virtually the entire belief system is problematic and contributes to severe abuse, psychological and spiritual. Understanding these religious abuses serves to highlight areas where abuses have occurred, helps to identify underlying neurophysiology, and hopefully provides insights to prevent such abuse in the future. Two prominent examples that are widely known are the polygamy practices of the Mormon Church and the child sexual abuse scandal of the Catholic Church.

The Church of Jesus Christ of Latter-day Saints, commonly known as the Mormon Church, has a complex history with instances of religious abuses that have affected individuals and communities. The practice of

---

135   Hassan S. *Combating Cult Mind Control: The #1 Best-Selling Guide to Protection, Rescue, and Recovery from Destructive Cults.* Freedom of Mind Press; 2018.

polygamy, especially during the nineteenth century, has been a controversial aspect of Mormon history.[136] Polygamy has overlaps with much of what we have previously discussed, in terms of sexual behaviors, as it implies that one man will have ongoing sexual relationships with multiple women. Some women in this tradition experience coercion, lack of agency, and emotional trauma in polygamous relationships. These women often feel compelled to be part of a group of many wives whether they want to or not. Of course, some women find polygamy acceptable and embrace it, while others suffer severe psychological trauma. The Mormon Church has also been particularly unkind to LGBTQ+ individuals and people of minorities. This has caused harm and discrimination against individuals who hold nontraditional sexual orientations and beliefs, resulting in social exclusion, emotional distress, and restricted access to religious rites.

The Catholic Church child sexual abuse scandal represents one of the most significant and disturbing cases of institutional abuse in modern history.[137] The hierarchical structure of the Catholic Church, coupled with a culture of secrecy and deference to authority, created an environment in which abusive behavior could flourish. Power imbalances between priests and vulnerable individuals, specifically children, coupled with a lack of accountability and transparency, enabled perpetrators to exploit their positions of trust.

The requirement of celibacy for Catholic priests has been identified as a contributing factor to the abuse scandal. The suppression of natural sexual urges may have led to the heightened expression of those desires in harmful and inappropriate ways, particularly when coupled with a lack of healthy outlets and support systems. Restricting normal sexual behaviors and feelings may have contributed to a kind of artificial hypersexuality— they would not have been hypersexual in the general society, but because of the heavy restrictions, it is likely some individuals were no longer able

136   Compton T. *In Sacred Loneliness: The Plural Wives of Joseph Smith*. Signature Books; 1997.

137   Reuters Staff. Pope Francis meets Irish abuse survivors. Reuters. 2018. https://www.reuters.com/article/us-pope-ireland-meeting/pope-francis-meets-irish-abuse-survivors-idUSKCN1LA0PD.

to control their normal sexual feelings. One can see the similarities in how religious and sexual abuses can intersect. And like sexual abuse, this can lead to various types of cognitive distortions, rationalizations, and justifications, which enable the specific individuals to perpetrate and perpetuate the abuse.

The failure of Church authorities to adequately respond to reports of abuse and hold perpetrators accountable allowed the problem to persist. Instances of cover-ups—moving priests to new locations without disclosing their histories—and a reluctance to involve secular authorities further perpetuated the cycle of abuse and shielded perpetrators from legal consequences.

The most significant consequence of the scandal is the profound and lasting impact on the victims. Survivors of abuse within the Catholic Church often experience a range of psychological, emotional, and physical consequences, including PTSD, depression, anxiety, and a loss of faith. Many victims struggle with trust, intimacy, and forming healthy relationships throughout their lives.

The revelations of widespread child sexual abuse and the subsequent mishandling of cases by Church authorities have significantly eroded public trust in the Catholic Church. The scandal has damaged the institution's moral authority and credibility, leading to declining church attendance, decreased donations, and a loss of influence in societal and political matters.

The scandal has prompted a reevaluation of the Church's policies and practices regarding child protection. Many dioceses have implemented stricter protocols for reporting allegations, background checks, and mandatory training. The establishment of independent review boards and the appointment of external auditors aim to ensure transparency and prevent future abuses.

It is interesting that such issues even had an impact on my own research. Through a chain of events, I came to find out that there had been accusations against prominent members of the OM group. Specifically, their originator and founder was arrested by the FBI on charges of forced labor. On one hand, this was very upsetting and disappointing to me regardless of the ultimate outcome (as of yet, there have been no convictions). No one should ever have to deal with abuse in any manner or from any source. I was disappointed because I had heard from so many people that the OM practice had benefited them. As it is for abuse within the Catholic Church, it is greatly unfortunate when people in power are able to take advantage through persuasion, coercion, and the powerful effects practices have on the mind and brain. But OM, like Catholicism, can have potential benefits as well, provided that no one is taken advantage of or abused. In the end, there are important psychological and neurological lessons to be learned about the great positives and negatives that can follow spiritual and sexual practices. Like the rituals that they incorporate, they can be used for great good or great evil.

CHAPTER 11

SEXUALITY, RELIGION, AND VIOLENCE

Completely destroy them—the Hittites, Amorites, Canaanites, Perizzites, Hivites and Jebusites—as the Lord your God has commanded you. Otherwise, they will teach you to follow all the detestable things they do in worshiping their gods, and you will sin against the Lord your God.

—Deuteronomy 20:17–18 (NIV)

RELIGION AND VIOLENCE: THE CRUSADES FACTOR

If the sexual and spiritual abuse we considered in the prior chapter represents the "dark side," then sexual and spiritual violence takes it to a whole new level. The relationship between religion and violence is a complex issue that has been debated by scholars, religious leaders, and political leaders for centuries. While some argue that religion is a source of peace and harmony, others point to extensive historical and contemporary examples of religiously motivated aggression and violence. With what we now know about the intimate relationship between the brain, sexuality, and spirituality, it makes sense to determine not only how religion and sexuality intersect with violence but also where all of these aspects of humanity arise within the human brain. Let us explore the various dimensions of this relationship, with a focus on the causes and consequences of religiously motivated violence.

Religion has been used to justify violence throughout history. For example, the Crusades, the Inquisition, and the Salem witch trials were all instances in which religion was used to justify violence against individuals or groups. Throughout history, Catholics and Protestants frequently fought as have the Muslims and Hindus, Jews and Muslims, and many other combinations of religious groups. In more recent times, religiously motivated violence has been carried out by extremist groups such as Al Qaeda and ISIS, who use religion to justify their acts of terrorism.[138] These groups often claim to be fighting for a religious cause, and they see violence as a legitimate means of achieving their objectives.

However, it is important to note that religion is not the sole cause of violence on a broader scale. Other factors such as economic inequality, political oppression, and cultural differences can also contribute to violence. In many cases, religion is used as a tool to mobilize people around a particular cause, rather than being the root cause of the violence itself. This is a fundamental distinction. Most religious wars, while pitting one ideology against another, usually came down to the egos and power interests of a select group of leaders, irrespective of specific religious views.

On the individual level, we might ponder how religion and violence connect in the human brain. Violence itself, or at least aggression, which is the precursor to violence, begins at the root of most nervous systems dating back hundreds of millions of years in virtually every animal. Even an amoeba will engulf its food in a destructive manner so that the amoeba can eat and have energy. As stated by Ray Dalio, "Life is a giant smorgasbord," and every form of life has to eat another form of life. Or in the case of plants, they at least have to take over a piece of land that squeezes out other plants. Thus, "violence," when defined as destroying or eliminating something else, occurs every minute of every day.

In most higher animals, we have already mentioned the fight or flight response associated with the autonomic nervous system. The operative word here is "fight." The autonomic nervous system gets all of the body's parts ready for the fight, but fighting engages more than just the autonomic nervous system. Muscle movement and coordination, as well as higher cognitive processes in mammals and primates, become an important part of violence.

---

138   Juergensmeyer M. *Terror in the Mind of God: The Global Rise of Religious Violence.* University of California Press; 2017; Moussalli AS. *Islamic Fundamentalism and the Gulf Crisis.* University Press of Florida; 1999.

The prefrontal cortex is one of the most important brain regions involved in violent behavior. This region is responsible for many higher cognitive functions, including decision-making, impulse control, and emotion regulation. Dysfunction in the prefrontal cortex has been linked to a range of violent behaviors, including impulsive aggression and criminal behavior. A brain imaging study of 41 murderers showed that these individuals who exhibited violent behavior had reduced activity in the prefrontal cortex compared to nonviolent individuals.[139] This suggests that dysfunction in this brain region may contribute to violent behavior.

Another important brain region that is involved in violent behavior is the amygdala.[140] The amygdala is responsible for processing emotions, including fear and anger. Dysfunction in this region has been linked to increased aggression and violence.[141] Studies have shown that individuals who exhibit violent behavior have increased activity in the amygdala compared to nonviolent individuals. This suggests that the amygdala may play a role in the heightened emotional arousal that is often associated with violent behavior.

The hippocampus is yet another brain region that is involved in violent behavior. The hippocampus is responsible for forming and retrieving memories and has been linked to a range of mental health disorders, including post-traumatic stress disorder. Studies have shown that individuals with PTSD, who often exhibit aggressive behavior, have reduced hippocampal volume compared to non-PTSD individuals.[142] Thus, dysfunction in the

---

139 Raine A, Buchsbaum M, LaCasse L. Brain abnormalities in murderers indicated by positron emission tomography. *Biol Psychiatry*. 1997;42(6):495-508.

140 Blair RJ. The amygdala and ventromedial prefrontal cortex: functional contributions and dysfunction in psychopathy. *Phil Trans Royal Soc B: Biol Sci*. 2008;363(1503):2557-2565.

141 Coccaro EF, McCloskey MS, Fitzgerald DA, Phan KL. Amygdala and orbitofrontal reactivity to social threat in individuals with impulsive aggression. *Biol Psychiatry*. 2007;62(2):168-178.

142 Bremner JD, Randall P, Vermetten E, et al. Magnetic resonance imaging-based measurement of hippocampal volume in posttraumatic stress disorder related to childhood physical and sexual abuse—a preliminary report. *Biol Psychiatry*. 1997;41(1):23-32.

hippocampus may contribute to the development of violent behavior in individuals with PTSD.

Violent behavior is a complex phenomenon that can be influenced by a variety of factors, including brain structure and function. The prefrontal cortex, amygdala, and hippocampus are all important brain regions that have been linked to violent behavior. Importantly, this complex of brain structures is also intimately involved in our social interactions with others. Through such mutual interactions, the tendency toward violence can quickly expand beyond the individual to larger groups of individuals.

One might wonder whether religious violence actually pays off in the end. There is certainly some evidence for this. Just like species that become more adaptive to a specific environment out compete and destroy other species, religions that are violent can also produce similar results. For example, the Crusades, which had the purported goal of recapturing the Holy Land from the Muslims, gave the Catholic Church an opportunity to assert its authority and influence over the Christian world as well. The Church played a crucial role in the Crusades, providing moral and financial support to the crusaders. The popes of the time also used the Crusades as a way to enhance their authority over the secular rulers of Europe. By calling for the Crusades and providing spiritual guidance to the crusaders, the popes were able to cement their position as the ultimate authority in matters of faith and morality.

The Crusades also helped to revive the papacy's prestige and power. Before the Crusades, the papacy was in a state of decline, with various secular powers competing for influence over the Church. However, the Crusades provided the papacy with an opportunity to reassert its authority and establish itself as the leader of the Christian world. The Crusades also helped to increase the papacy's financial resources, as the Church received donations and tithes from the crusaders and their supporters.

Finally, the Crusades led to the expansion of the Catholic Church's influence and power beyond Europe. The Crusades were not just fought in the Holy Land, but also in Spain, Portugal, and other parts of Europe. As the crusaders conquered new territories, they established Christian kingdoms and principalities, which were governed by the Church. This allowed the Catholic Church to expand its reach and influence beyond Europe into the Middle East and North Africa. And from an evolutionary perspective, this meant that the beliefs and the genetics that supported the Crusaders were more likely to survive and be passed on.[143]

Other religious wars have also brought power and influence to various religious groups over time. It appears that sometimes, mixing violence with religion in the right kind of setting can lead to long lasting adaptability of a given tradition which enables it to survive and perpetuate itself. Some have argued that religion greatly facilitates war by promoting a group belief system that strongly supports the "us versus them" mentality by providing a fever pitch intensity for fighting while dehumanizing enemies.[144] This seems consistent with what we know about how the brain works through rituals, originally designed for mating, to support the processes that lead to violence, and ultimately, group warfare.

SOCIAL INFLUENCES ON VIOLENCE

In one of the famous scenes from the science fiction movie, *2001: A Space Odyssey*, a group of prehuman primates is shown in which one of them discovers how to create a club from animal bones. But as soon as the one ape learns how to use the weapon, the others in the clan subsequently also learn to use it. This aspect of violence is particularly important in human beings who learned to be violent both as individuals and as groups. The ability to coordinate an attack was likely a particularly adaptive advantage utilizing the social parts of the brain to harness violent actions of individuals within the group. While initial violence might have been to kill prey, as is the case in many predatory species, it enabled certain *Homo* lineages to outcompete and kill off other species. Some have even suggested that human violence was a particularly adaptive trait that led to humanity ultimately taking over the planet.

The rituals we have discussed previously help to galvanize groups to work together and to keep violence at bay within the group by fostering

---

143   Kriegman D. *The Book of War*. Natural Selection Press, 2024.

144   Kriegman D. *The Book of War*. Natural Selection Press, 2024.

social cohesion and creating a sense of intragroup unity. This is why it is also true that religion has been a force for peace and reconciliation.[145] Many religious traditions emphasize the importance of compassion, forgiveness, and nonviolence among its followers. For example, the teachings of Jesus Christ emphasize love and forgiveness, while the principles of Buddhism emphasize nonviolence and peaceful coexistence. Many religious leaders and organizations have worked to promote peace and reconciliation, often using their religious beliefs as a source of inspiration.

At the core is the sense of oneness and connectedness, the primal feeling associated with sexual experience. Thus, sexual rituals bring together people for mating and religious and social rituals bring together people in cohesive societies. However, there is another side to how these rituals work. While they decrease intragroup conflict and violence, they increase intergroup conflict and violence.

How do the same rituals increase peace for a group while increasing violence between groups? What is important is what is included in the wholeness and connectedness of the rituals. For example, if just your family is included, you might be fighting off intruders or other groups trying to take your land and resources, protecting your family whom you feel close to. And if it is a larger group of people, say Christians, then there can be a great deal of animosity against people of other religions, even though you love your fellow Christians.

WHY DO WE CHOOSE US INSTEAD OF THEM?

There is an interesting reason that our brain feels aggression toward people and ideas that are not part of our group. You might have guessed that it comes down to how our brain operates. The issue is that our brain's mechanism for self-maintenance is one of the main ways our brain keeps us alive. As we have seen, religion provides an excellent source for supporting the brain's

---

145   Appleby RS. *The Ambivalence of the Sacred: Religion, Violence, and Reconciliation*. Rowman & Littlefield; 2000; Gopin M. *Between Eden and Armageddon: The Future of World Religions, Violence, and Peacemaking*. Oxford University Press; 2000.

self-maintenance function. But what if someone outside your group is telling you that you have gotten it wrong—that you don't understand how the world works and your ideas about morals, politics, or religion are in error?

When confronted with an alternative view of the world, your brain has one of two choices to make regarding survival: either you are right and the other person is wrong, or the other person is right and you are wrong. Which do you think your brain will choose? The majority of the time, your brain will conclude that you are right. After all, if you are wrong, your survival is in immediate danger! If you don't understand how the world works, then you are in a lot of trouble. Your arousal system and amygdala kick in, and you feel strong anxiety. To quell that anxiety, it is much easier for the brain to conclude that you really do know what is going on. Therefore, the other person or the other group must be wrong.

While that initial conclusion settles your brain, you are left with the disturbing issue that someone out there still says you are wrong. What should you do about that? First, you might try to argue your point. You might try to convince the other person that your beliefs are right and they are wrong. In religious terms, you are trying to proselytize and convert them. But their brain is doing the same thing as yours so they will likely defend their own beliefs.

From your brain's perspective, though, you must begin to conclude that not only are they wrong but also maybe there is something inherently bad about them. Maybe they have a mental disorder, or worse, maybe they are truly evil. After all, why would they keep insisting that their beliefs are right, when you "know" they are wrong?

If they are evil, you have reduced them from being another human being with different ideas to an evil and horrible creature, not even human, who probably should be destroyed. By reducing other people and other groups to nonhuman, evil objects, committing violence against them becomes a lot easier. So, all of the mechanisms that have gotten into your brain, from mating rituals to sexual rituals to the social cohesion, create that strong sense of connectedness with your group and your beliefs, but lead to potentially devastating violence with other groups.

On the other hand, your beliefs, myths, and rituals might foster a deeper understanding of the differences between your group and another.

For example, perhaps you will come to the conclusion that all human beings are created by God in God's image. Even if they have different beliefs, even evil beliefs, you might have a greater sense of compassion for those that oppose you because they are still created in God's image. As admonished in Matthew 5:43-45 (NIV): "You have heard that it was said, 'Love your neighbor and hate your enemy.' But I tell you, love your enemies and pray for those who persecute you, that you may be children of your Father in heaven."

In a similar manner, religion can play a positive role in conflict resolution. Religious leaders and organizations have often played a key role in bringing together conflicting parties and facilitating dialogue and negotiation, basing their approaches on the positive emotions that derive from those traditions. For example, the role of religious leaders in the peace process in Northern Ireland was critical in bringing an end to the years of conflict there.

CONVERSIONS AND BREAKUPS

Another similarity between religion and sexuality has to do with when people switch allegiances. Religious conversions are a prominent example. For whatever reason, the person realizes that they no longer feel the same way about their current belief system and changes their entire way of thinking about that religion. The prior beliefs, rituals, and behaviors associated with the first religion are now viewed as wrong. Since the prior beliefs are no longer part of the new sense of oneness, those previously intense beliefs are flipped completely around and are viewed as wrong or evil. The person not only begins to follow the new religion but typically has to substantially reject those prior beliefs as unreal. This can lead to great animosity or even violence against one's prior religious group.

In sex and love, there are often many times in a person's life when breakups occur. For whatever reason, the person realizes that they no longer feel the same way and changes their entire way of thinking about the other person. When young, these can be devastating at first, but usually people move on relatively quickly. When people are married for many years, and perhaps have children, there are many times that the intense love and connection that was once felt is flipped completely around, leading to substantial hurt and anger, aggression, and even violence. It seems that divorced individuals frequently have great animosity for each other, which always seems a bit strange given that they once loved each other. What happened? When that sense of inclusiveness is destroyed, as we discussed above, that person is now cast out of the sense of oneness and becomes associated with a different part of reality. The person can be viewed as bad, evil, or even unhuman. While sometimes this animosity can resolve over time through processing feelings, it is often very difficult to reconcile in a meaningful way.

In both circumstances, the self-maintenance function of the brain has to decide which belief system to follow in order to ensure proper understanding of the world. Most of the time, people stick with their prevailing belief system. But when they have to switch, either because it is forced upon them—such as their spouse breaking up with them—or because they realize that there is a new and better belief system, then the brain has a need to reject the old one. And since the brain needs one view of reality, rejecting the old belief system is a philosophical and existential necessity.

SEXUALITY AND VIOLENCE

The relationship between sex and violence requires careful consideration, especially when it comes to understanding religion and violence. While there is no definitive answer to the question of how sex and violence are related, there are a number of factors that have been identified as playing a role in this relationship. And each of these relates to various brain processes that are linked to both sexuality and violence.

Interestingly, the very small and very ancient part of the brain, the hypothalamus is where sexuality and violence both reside. To be more specific, the ventrolateral region of the ventromedial hypothalamus acts as a hub for both sex and violence. The neurons are so close together that it certainly seems understandable how sexuality and violence can overlap. Just move a few neurons one way or the other, and a person can easily confuse violence and sexuality. Perhaps this is a large part of the reason that there is such an intense relationship between violence and sexuality.

A most basic analysis of the act of sex reveals that it is inherently a "violent" act. It is the male penetrating the female, and in the most sensitive and private of areas. It is hoped that in the majority of cases this action is ultimately welcomed by the female. But there are many times that such penetration is not a welcome act, and instead, is an act of sexual assault.

Individually, research shows that people who combine sexuality with aggression and violence exhibit brain abnormalities. Studies of pedophiles, sex offenders, and rapists reveal abnormalities in brain regions involved in reward, motivation, and moral judgment. This likely leads these aggressive sexual people to be both over-responsive to sexual reward stimuli and also to make inappropriate moral decisions.[146] In other words, they react more strongly to sexual stimuli, and they can't control their behaviors in response to those stimuli. There are even some unusual neurological conditions in which people have damage to their limbic system or in Parkinson's patients in which they lose the ability to control their behaviors leading to excessive and aggressive sexual behaviors.

When it comes to large groups, one of the most well-known examples of combining sex and violence involves sexual violence during war. Dating back to antiquity, rape has been used as a weapon against opponents. Rape humiliates the enemy and strikes fear into the population with the goal of making it easier to conquer a given group. But it is also interesting how possessed of sex an invading army might become, raping many of the women in the group of conquered people. Historians throughout time have noted this disturbing link between physical violence and sex.

Historian Gerda Lerner stated that, "The practice of raping the women of a conquered group has remained a feature of warfare and conquest from the second millennium BC to the present. It is a social practice which, like the torture of prisoners, has been resistant to 'progress,' to humanitarian reforms, and to sophisticated moral and ethical considerations. I suggest

---

146   Chen CY, Raine A, Chou KH, Chen IY, Hung D, Lin CP. Abnormal white matter integrity in rapists as indicated by diffusion tensor imaging. *BMC Neurosci*. 2016;17(1):45. doi:10.1186/s12868-016-0278-3.

this is the case because it is a practice built into and essential to the structure of patriarchal institutions and inseparable from them. It is at the beginning of the system, prior to class formation, that we can see this in its purest essence."[147]

I would argue that it is likely the overlapping sexual and violent areas of the brain that have resulted in armies throughout time, from the Romans to the Huns to the Mongols to the present day, to engage in conquest rape. These areas are so close together that stimulating the sexual part can potentially stimulate the violence part and vice versa. Thus, when an army is finished with their fight, all of that aggression is likely to foment a great deal of sexual energy. This energy gets directed at the enemy leading to the horrors of conquest rape.

From an evolutionary perspective, it could be argued that rape, along with the violent elimination of mate competitors, is the most aggressive way of passing on one's genes to future generations, and in this way, is an adaptive trait. In fact, data suggest that 1 in 200 males in the world have a unique Y chromosome lineage that traces back to Genghis Khan.[148] Such a finding is likely the result of his armies killing off many other male lineages while supporting the survival of their own. And there are a number of other lineages that also trace back to specific individuals or groups who led violent escapades around the world. While there are many moral and philosophical problems with such an approach, there clearly is an evolutionary survival impact.

The question of whether violence is an adaptation is a controversial topic that has been debated by scholars for many years. Some argue that violence is an innate behavior that has evolved over time to serve a specific purpose, while others believe that it is a learned behavior that is the result of environmental factors.

Proponents of the theory that violence is an adaptation argue that it has evolved as a means of survival in many circumstances. According to this view, violence can be seen as a form of competition where individuals use aggression

---

147   Lerner G. *The Creation of Patriarchy*. Oxford University Press; 1987.

148   Zerjal T, Xue Y, Bertorelle G, et al. The genetic legacy of the Mongols. *Am J Hum Genet.* 2003;72(3):717-721.

to gain access to resources such as food, mates, and territory.[149] This behavior has been observed in many animal species, including chimpanzees, lions, and wolves, in which males will fight over access to females and territory.

There is also biological evidence to suggest that human aggression has evolved as an adaptation. For example, studies have found that individuals with high levels of testosterone, a hormone associated with aggression, are more likely to engage in violent behavior.[150] This suggests that aggression may have been selected for in human evolution as a means of competing for mates and resources.

However, some have questioned the idea that violence is an evolutionary adaptation. One major critique is that the prevalence of violence varies widely across cultures and historical periods, suggesting that it is not a universal behavior.[151] However, if you recall that the nature of evolutionary traits requires a range of abilities or aspects of that trait, it makes sense that some people are more and some people are less violently inclined. Unfortunately, it seems an undeniable fact that on the evolutionary playing field, a violent group is much more likely to kill off a nonviolent group.

Of course, there needs to be sufficient nonviolence within the group to maintain itself. In other words, too much violence within a group will destabilize it so that there needs to be a way to create out-group aggression and in-group peace. Interestingly, as we have considered above, rituals have the ability to do both at the same time. Rituals create a sense of group cohesion for everyone involved in the ritual and cast an aggressive or violent stance toward anyone not participating. This also helps us understand the relationship between sexuality and violence. Sexuality within the group contributes to social bonding and thus, sex can bring people together. But sexuality can also be used as a tool for violence. Religious and spiritual rituals are also likely to be particularly effective for creating compassion within the group and exacting

149 Wilson M, Daly M. Life expectancy, economic inequality, homicide, and reproductive timing in Chicago neighbourhoods. *British Med J.* 1997;314(7089):1271-1274.

150 Archer J. Testosterone and human aggression: an evaluation of the challenge hypothesis. *Neurosci Biobehavior Rev.* 2006;30(3):319-345.

151 Wrangham R, Peterson D. *Demonic Males: Apes and the Origins of Human Violence.* Houghton Mifflin; 1996.

violence outside of the group. The Bible is replete with stories of how the Jews or Christians come together against other groups that do not believe in God.

WHAT FACTORS GENERALLY CONNECT SEXUALITY AND VIOLENCE?

Present-day research has identified several factors as contributing to violence being connected to sexuality, starting with pornography. Is it possible that the factors we describe below have an impact on the hypothalamus cells that cause overlap between neuronal activity in the violence and sexual neurons? Some studies have found that exposure to violent pornography can lead to aggressive behavior, including sexual violence.[152] The relationship between pornography and violence is multifaceted, and there is ongoing debate about whether pornography actually causes violence. But we know that the more the brain is primed with certain types of information, particularly when it is emotional or sexual, the stronger those ideas and responses become.

Another factor that has been linked to the relationship between sex and violence is childhood abuse. Research has shown that individuals who have experienced childhood abuse are more likely to engage in violent behavior, including sexual violence, later in life.[153] This link between childhood abuse and violent behavior is not limited to sexual violence and has been observed across a range of violent behaviors. It is possible that childhood abuse leads to sexual violence because abuse itself causes massive reactions in the autonomic nervous system, which is controlled by the hypothalamus along with the stress hormone cortisol.[154]

---

152 Malamuth NM, Addison T, Koss M. Pornography and sexual aggression: are there reliable effects and can we understand them? *Ann Rev Sex Res.* 2000;11(1):26-91.

153 Fergusson DM, Horwood LJ, Lynskey MT. Childhood sexual abuse and psychiatric disorder in young adulthood: II. Psychiatric outcomes of childhood sexual abuse. *J Amer Acad Child Adolesc Psychiatr.* 1997;36(12):1666-1674.

154 De Bellis MD, Chrousos GP, Dorn LD, et al. Hypothalamic-pituitary-adrenal axis dysregulation in sexually abused girls. *J Clin Endocrinol Metab.* 1994;78(2):249-255. doi:10.1210/jcem.78.2.8106608.

In addition, some researchers have identified a link between sexual objectification and violence. Sexual objectification occurs when individuals are treated as objects or commodities rather than as human beings. We have also seen how various rituals can lead participants to view nonparticipants as being "outside" of reality and therefore evil, objectifying them in a way that facilitates violence against them. This can happen in a range of other contexts including the media, advertising, and popular culture. Some researchers have argued that sexual objectification can lead to an increased likelihood of violent behavior, including sexual violence.[155] These changes also result in lower levels of oxytocin in the hypothalamus.[156] Remember that oxytocin helps people bond to others, so a deficiency of oxytocin is likely to result in problems with establishing intimate relationships.

While low oxytocin might make a person less connected to others and therefore more aggressive, research also has shown that oxytocin, like rituals, can have both prosocial and antisocial effects, depending on the context in which it is released.[157] For example, while oxytocin can increase feelings of trust, empathy, and bonding, it can also lead to increased aggression toward out-group members. After all, if you feel very close to your spouse or child, you are more likely to protect them, violently if necessary. Oxytocin might make the in-group versus out-group response much stronger.

Other researchers have suggested that the connection between sex and violence in the brain may be related to a broader tendency toward sensation-seeking behavior. Sensation-seeking is a personality trait characterized by a desire for novel and intense experiences. It has been linked to a range of risky behaviors, including drug use, gambling, and high-risk sexual behavior. Research has further shown that sensation-seeking behavior is

---

155 Bartky SL. *Femininity and Domination: Studies in the Phenomenology of Oppression.* Routledge; 1990.

156 Veenema AH, Bredewold R, Neumann ID. Opposite effects of maternal separation on intermale and maternal aggression in C57BL/6 mice: link to hypothalamic vasopressin and oxytocin immunoreactivity. *Psychoneuroendocrinol.* 2007;32(5):437-450. doi:10.1016/j.psyneuen.2007.02.008.

157 Bartz JA, Zaki J, Bolger N, Ochsner KN. Social effects of oxytocin in humans: context and person matter. *Trends Cogn Sci.* 2011;15(7):301-309.

associated with alterations in brain function and structure.[158] Specifically, sensation-seekers have been found to have reduced activity in brain regions associated with impulse control and decision-making, and increased activity in brain regions associated with reward and motivation.

Research has shown that testosterone, a hormone associated with aggression, is present in higher levels in individuals who commit sexual offenses.[159] However, it is important to note that not all individuals with high levels of testosterone engage in violent behavior, and there are many other neurological factors that can influence the relationship between hormones and behavior.

One area of research that sheds light on the connection between sex and violence in the brain is neuroimaging. A study conducted by researchers at the University of Pennsylvania found that other than the hypothalamus, there is another brain area that is involved in both sexual and aggressive behavior.[160] The study found that activity in the ventromedial prefrontal cortex, a brain region involved in processing reward and motivation, was associated with both sexual and aggressive behavior. In addition, this area of the frontal lobe is connected to the hypothalamus and amygdala, suggesting that there may be a common neural basis for these two types of behavior.[161]

All of these factors mentioned above affect brain areas that are involved in sexuality and violence, as well as the rituals that contribute to how human beings behave. As we have considered all along, rituals lead to that sense of connectedness, but only to the group or the myth that is involved with that connectedness. We can feel connected to our family, our community, our country, or all of humanity.

If we look at one more issue that particularly links sexuality and

---

158 Zuckerman M. Sensation seeking and the brain. *Behav Brain Sci.* 2007; 30(5-6):415-416.

159 Archer J. Testosterone and human aggression: an evaluation of the challenge hypothesis. *Neurosci Biobehavior Rev.* 2006;30(3):319-345.

160 Berkowitz L, Harmon-Jones E. Toward an understanding of the determinants of anger. *Emotion.* 2004;4(2):107-130.

161 Hashikawa Y, Hashikawa K, Falkner AL, Lin D. Ventromedial hypothalamus and the generation of aggression. *Front Syst Neurosci.* 2017;11:94. doi:10.3389/fnsys.2017.00094.

violence, it has to do with the extent to which rituals define the in-group and the out-group. By this I mean that everyone or everything that is contained within the group involved with the ritual is considered to be the in-group. But this means it is not just about the people; it is about the entire mythos that binds the group together. This can be incorporated into the group's ethnicity, location, and their beliefs. Thus, the group is connected by their beliefs surrounding things such as politics, morals, and religion.

When one surveys the unbelievable and horrific violence humanity has rendered on itself over the millennia, it certainly makes sense that sexuality, spirituality, and violence are all deeply rooted in the brain. It seems that it is almost a neurological imperative to blend sexuality and spirituality with violence, primarily through various rituals. Fortunately, there is also the opportunity to foster compassion and love. However, these positive feelings often require the higher parts of our brain—the frontal lobe and parietal lobe—to help us find ways of balancing the aggressive and violent aspects of our species. These parts of the brain help us balance our aggressive tendencies by providing a set of rules and morals that foster forgiveness, compassion, and behaviors that support a cohesive community.

CHAPTER 12

SEXUALITY AND THE DEVELOPMENT OF MORALITY

Lust is the source of all our actions, and humanity.

—Blaise Pascal, Pensées

"Food for the stomach and the stomach for food, and God will destroy them both." The body, however, is not meant for sexual immorality but for the Lord, and the Lord for the body.

—1 Corinthians 6:13 (NIV)

RELIGION, POLITICS, AND MORALS

At the beginning of this book, one of the things that we considered was how religion and spirituality might form a set of morals that would be useful for maintaining a cohesive and stable society. In this way, religious and spiritual beliefs can have a survival advantage by enabling a strong social group to develop. Perhaps more important, this moral and societal benefit hopefully offsets the negative aspects of religion and spirituality that are part of their dark side. In fact, we might expect that evolution would lead to a balance between the positive and adaptive aspects of religion compared to the negative and maladaptive aspects. After all, if religion ultimately was more problematic than it was worth, it probably would not have survived and flourished for thousands of years.

Certainly, early civilizations relied heavily on their religious beliefs for supporting the leader as a king or pharaoh who has God-given abilities and a station to lead the society. In all ancient societies, it was believed that God, or a group of gods, were responsible for endowing the leader with intelligence, compassion, and strength. For example, the Egyptian pharaohs were denoted by Horus, the falcon God. Part of the morality that developed around the leader was a strong sense of worship and loyalty. By paying homage to the gods, members of the society were willing to work for, slave for, and fight for the king or queen. But this also helps to support society as a whole by fighting against enemies and fending off attackers with religious fervor.

Religion has continued to influence political systems up to the present day. Thomas Jefferson invoked the importance of inalienable rights "endowed by a Creator," placing that additional emphasis of religion on the fundamental rights of human beings—life, liberty, and the pursuit of happiness.

It is often challenging to separate religion from politics even though one of the stated goals of many political ideologies is to keep church and state distinct. On the other hand, many of today's political groups specifically embrace religious and spiritual ideals. To date, all US presidents have ended their speeches with "God bless America."

But if religion plays a prominent role in political systems, and ultimately the rules and morals that govern them, we must ask the question as to where those rules and morals come from? Is it possible that just as religion appears to derive from the same biological underpinnings of sexuality, so too morality derives from many basic sexual and mating concepts?

In *Sex at Dawn*, a fascinating survey of human sexuality in prehistory, Christopher Ryan and Cacilda Jethá argue that there was a pervasive egalitarianism among our early ancestors.[162] This included their sexual habits: "A great deal of research from primatology, anthropology, anatomy, and psychology points to the same fundamental conclusion: human beings and our hominid ancestors have spent almost all of the past few million years or so in small, intimate bands in which adults had several sexual relationships at any given time. This approach to sexuality probably persisted until the

---

162   Ryan C, Jetha C. *Sex at Dawn: The Prehistoric Origins of Modern Sexuality*. Harper Collins; 2010.

rise of agriculture and private property no more than ten thousand years ago. In addition to voluminous scientific evidence, many explorers, missionaries, and anthropologists support this view, having penned accounts rich with tales of orgiastic rituals, unflinching mate sharing, and an open sexuality unencumbered by guilt or shame." At some point, there was likely a reasonable amount of sharing of mates, at least within a given group of people. They support this argument by pointing to female chimps and bonobos, which have sex dozens of times a day with the willing males in the group. They go on to argue that in tight tribal communities, parental investment in children tends to be diffuse, mitigating what noted writer Robert Ardrey has called our "territorial imperative".

Even in what may have been the egalitarian environments of early humans it's hard to imagine there weren't complications. Perhaps in these early tribal societies of small groups our more aggressive-possessive traits were not as pronounced. Perhaps in some environments they simply didn't develop? But did they completely disappear? In any event, with the advent of agriculture around 10,000 years ago, as Ryan and Jethá point out, whatever egalitarian tendencies we possessed dropped away, supplanted by something else. There was now ownership of land and resources, and this led to protecting our possessions, and ultimately the families and mates of those family members. Thus, there was likely a balance that was formed at each stage of human evolutionary development that weighed the sharing of resources and individuals among a group, with the ownership and protection of that group. In a similar manner, this balance coincides with the balance we have considered regarding the need for peace and cohesion of a group with violence and aggression against other groups.

Remember, having a group can be inclusive and beneficial, but it can also lead to exclusivity and even violent and hateful behaviors. From a survival perspective, the important question, evolutionarily speaking, is how large a group are we interested in maintaining. Most people want to keep a strong family, and some broaden it to a local community, and from there, connect with a larger nation or all of humanity. At each level, there is a balance that needs to be maintained between what is considered included in and what is excluded from the group. This ultimately comes down to the mating process and who you include or exclude from that process. From the aforementioned points, it seems that sometimes that balance is weighted toward inclusivity while other times exclusivity.[163] From an evolutionary perspective, both can be adaptive, but it probably depends on how the environment pushes people to work together. A million years ago when food and shelters were found everywhere, the balance tilted toward sharing. But when food and shelters became more limited and exclusive, so did people.

This likely led to general rules and approaches towards sustaining family closeness and having mates that could maintain long-term relationships that were part of the overall inclusivity of the group. These rules were based on more basic biological principles that had to do with mate selection and how the brain operates. The biological principles include the importance of mate bonding and child bonding that is fostered in large part by oxytocin. The male's strength and violence used to defend a mate likely results from the testosterone that flows during mate selection and arousal. This also is tied into the autonomic nervous system's fight or flight response that leads to revenge behaviors. And finally, the resolution of various breaches of the rules and the protection of the self and family lead to feelings of calm and peacefulness. How do these various biological processes and the rules involved with mating and the protection of mates and the family lead to the fundamental elements of human morality?

THE BEGINNING OF MORALS

For this section, perhaps it is best to start with one of the most famous sets of ancient moral dictums, the Ten Commandments. Is it possible that the Commandments are essentially built out of basic sexual mores? For example, it is important not to covet someone else's mate, which was extended to not coveting anything else of your neighbor's. It is important not to commit adultery, a sexual act, which is analogous to not stealing another person's mate. If stealing a mate is bad, perhaps stealing other objects is equally immoral—hence, thou shalt not steal. Even the "Golden Rule" to

163   Newberg AB. Identity and the brain: the biological basis of our self. *Zygon*. 2023. https:// doi.org/10.1111/zygo.12873.

"do unto others as you would have them do unto you" seems based on not wanting others to steal your mate or injure your family. We should honor our mother and father, primarily because of the sexual relationship that led to our birth. And in the same vein, we should respect our elders just like young bucks must respect older alpha males.

The most important commandments have to do with worshiping God. In all human societies, and most mammalian species, there is an alpha male or female that all of the others must "bow down" to in order to adequately maintain the stability of the social hierarchy. Worshiping things is therefore deeply rooted in our biology and our brain. We want to feel taken care of and feel love so we should express those feelings as part of a broader moral context. It seems that most formal moral systems derive from basic ways in which we respect the mates of our fellow human beings, along with the mating hierarchy.

Let us look a bit closer at this fascinating issue that arises from our exploration of sexuality and spirituality and where morality fits in. When considering the rituals that surround mating, we have to acknowledge that there is a regulatory mechanism involved. There are rules to mating. One just does not go and have sex with someone, unless of course we are talking about rape, and we will discuss this issue shortly. Usually, you must follow the rules, which include all of the complex patterned behaviors, and eventually a sense of what the other individual is thinking and feeling. I have argued that mating rituals ultimately bind two animals together. On one hand, this happens spatially. But there is more involved than just two bodies coming together. The mystique of love is a fundamental component of mating. It is essential to be able to read another person and know what they are thinking and feeling. Are they receptive? Are they avoiding us? And perhaps most important: Is this a safe person as well as someone with whom I would like to have children with?

These latter two questions are quite important. Safety is always an issue and fundamental to our moral selves. If we do not feel safe, our very survival, and the survival of our genes, is in jeopardy. Morality enables people to feel safe with one another by enabling a fair playing field. If we do not trust another person, or if they act in immoral ways, such as stealing from us or hurting us, we recognize them as morally corrupt and will most likely try to avoid them as much as possible, or perhaps even punish them.

As the human brain developed, moral reasoning went beyond just the basic rules of mating rituals. Especially with the development of the frontal lobes and emotional areas (particularly the insula), we acquired empathy and a sense of another person's mind. We could understand what other people were thinking and feeling because we could extrapolate and project our own feelings onto them. From the basic notion of mate safety came a number of our moral concepts.

Interestingly, the morals that derive from the male and female are slightly different. The male develops morals to protect his genes for being passed on. On the male side, mating leads to the goal of protecting oneself and making sure that someone does not steal your mate from you. From an evolutionary perspective, this helps to ensure for the male that his genes are the ones that are indeed being passed on to the next generation. The woman knows that the baby is hers, but the man is never sure so he wants as best as possible to protect what he thinks are his offspring. The woman wants to protect herself and her baby, since this will also protect her genes from passing on to future generations.

From these rudimentary types of morals, human beings can extrapolate a full range of ethics. To begin with, it becomes wrong to take away someone else's mate, especially in a monogamously oriented group in which a mating pair is clearly established. As mentioned above, stealing someone's mate is stealing their future reproductive success. The male does not want to lose the opportunity to create offspring with a female he has selected as beneficial for the survival of his genes and offspring. The female wants to be able to ensure that the mate she thinks is best is the one she gets to mate with and give the best opportunity for survival of her offspring.

This latter point is important because one of the most egregiously immoral acts is rape. In rape, it steals a female from the male (or a male from a female in the case of male rape) who has previously bonded with her or had potential mating interest in her. And if the female rape victim becomes pregnant, rape essentially forces her to have offspring that she personally has not selected for. And of course, the greatest issue of all is the personal assault on the rape victim's body, which is emotionally and physically damaging in profound ways.

If it is wrong to steal a mate either physically through rape or strategically by charming a person psychologically or emotionally, then perhaps it is wrong to steal other things. After all, stealing resources such as food, water, and shelter can damage a person's survival and the survival of any progeny. And if it is important to maintain personal safety, perhaps it is important to maintain the safety of the group or community as well as the resources that are part of that community. When it comes to resources, morality often provides dictums about compensation. In fact, the commandments in the Bible extend beyond the first ten. We saw earlier the biblical rule that "whoever steals an ox or a sheep and slaughters it or sells it must pay back five head of cattle for the ox and four sheep for the sheep" (Exodus 22:1, NIV). This shows that there is compensation to help alleviate the effects of an immoral act. The ultimate hope of establishing such moral laws is to support the survival of individuals and the group.

Morals also develop from some of the fundamental tenets of a religion in terms of helping people follow and maintain their spiritual paths. In Buddhism and Hinduism, the goal of the religion is to achieve enlightenment. Rules and morals reflect on how to help everyone achieve that goal. Similarly, in monotheistic traditions, many of the morals focus on helping people lead a good and productive life. Morals in these traditions also stem from the notion of worshiping the ultimate leader—in this case, God. In many animal species in which there is an alpha male or queen, the rules governing how subordinates respond to that leader and the hierarchical structure of the group are more physically oriented through fights and displays. In human beings, these strategies become more elaborate but still derive from the fundamental maintenance of the hierarchy.

Thus, the elaboration of mating and sexual experience into the more complex human brain led not only to spirituality but to morality as well. Further, it may help us understand why spirituality and morality are so intimately linked. All religions provide a sense of morals and ethics by which we live our life based on sexuality and mating. Women want to feel protected and so developed the morality of personal protection, while men want to protect their genes and to have resources to protect those genes. It is remarkable how much has evolved from the "simple" act of the mating process.

It is interesting that important emotional responses associated with morality are also connected with the mating process. For example, shame and guilt become an integral part of mating as people interact. You feel embarrassed or ashamed if you do something "wrong" in the mating process. Sometimes this is a minor wrongdoing in the sense that you just don't make the right connection with someone. But other times, there is actual harm or injury that occurs, and a person is shunned by a potential mate, or sometimes even the larger group. Animals clearly display shame and embarrassment. Anyone who has ever owned a dog knows how they cower and hide when they have done something wrong that they know will disappoint their owner. People's brains work the same way. This is part of the mating process to assess who is included and who is excluded in the mating process. It also tells people how to navigate the mating process and particularly the hierarchical order of the group. This is the proverbial concept of whether that person is "in your league" or not. If you are rejected, you don't keep coming back because the embarrassment you feel makes you avoid that person and go after a different potential mate. If you did not experience this embarrassment, you might continue to try for the wrong mate, leading to instability in the group and greater aggression or violence. By withdrawing when rejected, it keeps the whole process and social structure moving smoothly.

REVENGE VERSUS FORGIVENESS

One final perspective (at least for now) on morality in humans comes from how we respond when there is a breach of moral behavior. If someone injures us, we typically have three routes to go in terms of our response:

We can try to seek revenge to equalize the wrong that has been done.
We can attempt to move past the wrong by ignoring it, if it is not particularly consequential (e.g., if someone steals $10 from you, it might be easier to let it go rather than spend the effort to rectify such a small incursion).
We can try to forgive the individual.
Both revenge and forgiveness find their sources in our biology but in

very different ways. I first discussed the neuropsychology of forgiveness 20 years ago. But now that we can consider sexuality as part of the moral process, we can relook at forgiveness.

In our initial discussion of forgiveness, we realized that an individual first has to recognize that an injury has occurred. But this is not so straightforward as it depends a lot on the social hierarchy.[164] If a boss yells at you for making a mistake, that might be an appropriate injury to receive. In fact, they are probably being mean in the hopes that you will do better next time. On the other hand, a boss is not allowed to abuse a subordinate. As part of the mating and social hierarchy, our brain recognizes a kind of balance with every other person. Some people rank higher than us and some lower. Depending on our relationship, we might have different responses to any given injury. As mentioned above, if you are an average looking guy, being scoffed at by a beautiful woman who is "out of your league" might not seem unreasonable. Our brain establishes these interpersonal balances and then helps us evaluate the behaviors in relation to that balance. If someone compliments us, our balance improves, and we feel a surge of dopamine that makes us feel happy and proud. If someone criticizes us, our amygdala fires and our sympathetic nervous system kicks in to make us feel upset or hurt. These mechanisms tell us which direction our overall status is affected by another person's behavior.

Our brain strives to maintain balance among the other people in our group as well as strive for ways to optimize our own standing. This is important for maintaining the social hierarchy which ultimately affects who mates with who. If someone compliments us, we might compliment them back. In so doing, we reestablish the balance. We have made both of us feel a bit more positive. On the other hand, when we perceive an injurious behavior, we have a tendency to want to injure the person back in order to restore the balance. If they insult us, we might insult them back.

This is the basis for the famous Lex Talionis: an eye for an eye. And this is described in many sacred texts from Hammurabi's Code to the Bible.

---

164   Newberg AB, d'Aquili EG, Newberg SK, DeMarici V. The neuropsychological basis of forgiveness. In: McCullough ME, Pargament KI, Thoresen CE, eds. *Forgiveness: Theory, Practice, and Research*. The Guilford Press; 2000.

Moral systems throughout history have relied on the restoring of interpersonal balance. But there is a problem with revenge behavior, particularly when it gets out of control. We always feel our own hurt more than we feel another's. That is because our own brain knows and feels our own emotions much more intensely compared to another's. But if each of us feels our own pain more than someone else's and if we are injured by that person and want to respond we are likely to respond with a worse injury than the initial one. We feel the hurt more, so we subsequently hurt the other person back more. But their brain goes through the same thing and this is how escalation occurs. One can see this type of revenge escalation happening all around the globe.

So, is there an off-ramp in this process? How do we extricate ourselves from a process which could lead to serious injury or death and which could also lead to destabilization of the group as a result of friends and family coming to the defense of the two involved individuals? The answer is forgiveness.

Forgiveness does something very unique—it de-escalates a situation and helps to restore balance without the need for revenge. Forgiveness occurs when the injured person reconciles that injury through a thought and emotional process that redefines the balance between the two people. This can happen in several possible ways. Perhaps the injured person reflects on times that they wronged someone and recognizes that all people make mistakes. Or perhaps there is a religious perspective taken—that we are all God's children, and we are all imperfect. Whatever conclusion the injured person comes to, it reestablishes the balance in their own mind and enables them to move forward while maintaining order. This is supported by previously conducted research revealing that forgiveness frequently elicits positive support for the forgiving individual.[165] Historically, many people converted to Christianity because the early Christians forgave their enemies. Such behavior, frequently from martyrs, helped propel Christianity to a popular place in the world.

---

165   Newberg AB, d'Aquili EG, Newberg SK, DeMarici V. The neuropsychological basis of forgiveness. In: McCullough ME, Pargament KI, Thoresen CE, eds. *Forgiveness: Theory, Practice, and Research*. The Guilford Press; 2000.

Forgiveness-like behaviors are found in a number of animal species also as a way of maintaining social balance. And importantly, forgiveness is associated with basic sexual hormones such as testosterone and oxytocin. Interestingly, oxytocin, which causes pair bonding, sometimes can make forgiveness less likely.[166] The reason is that the stronger the bond you form, and the stronger the sense of trust, the greater is the injury when that trust is broken. That makes forgiveness more difficult. Testosterone also can have a bit of an opposite effect. On one hand, testosterone makes people more aggressive, but it also makes them more vigilant, paying attention to potential injuries and thereby adaptively helping to prevent them in the first place.[167] Ultimately, forgiveness, as well as morality, has a lot to do with the social areas of the brain, areas of the brain that are involved in empathy and compassion as much as they are about sexuality and spirituality.

166   Yao S, Zhao W, Cheng R, Geng Y, Luo L, Kendrick KM. Oxytocin makes females, but not males, less forgiving following betrayal of trust. *Int J Neuropsychopharm.* 2014;17(11):1785-1792. https://doi.org/10.1017/S146114571400090X.

167   Khattak N, Habib SH, Durrani S, Rahman UU, Zeeshan N, Seema S. Comparison of serum testosterone levels among students studying in religious institutions and nonreligious institutions. *J Ayub Med Coll Abbottabad.* 2020;32(4):531-534.

CHAPTER 13

COMPASSION, SEX, AND THE BRAIN

The problem is, for men and women, the idea that sexuality is about dominance and submission, when, in fact, cooperation is a lot more fun, to put it my way. So, some of it, a lot of it, is just about empathy.

—Gloria Steinem

SEXUALITY AND RELIGION REVISITED

The rules and morals that arise out of how we manage our mating behaviors likely coevolved with the more profoundly positive aspects of sexuality and the deep bonds and relationships that we establish through mating.

I mentioned in the beginning of this book that many religious traditions tend to look negatively upon sexuality. That is not altogether accurate. Even the staunchest puritanical religious systems acknowledge that sexuality is a fundamental "glue" for marriage. And most perspectives in the monotheistic traditions recognize that sex, at least within marriage, and for procreation, is a reflection of God's love. For example, Pope John Paul II stated, "The body, and it alone, is capable of making visible what is invisible: the spiritual and divine." [168] For him, the sexual act of a married couple is an almost perfect image of the unity and communion of God in mutual love, whereby they give themselves in a total way—exclusively to one another. And through this marriage, sexuality leads to a fruitful and

---

168   West C. *Theology Of The Body For Beginners.* Ascension Press; 2004.

generous way of creating a new human being. Pope John Paul II stressed that there is great beauty in sexual love when done in the harmony of marriage supporting human values of a freely chosen total commitment and giving of the self to another. This type of sexual love is a kind of worship and an experience of the sacred.[169]

Judaism and Islam also recognize sexuality within marriage as a beautiful event and of fundamental importance in maintaining a healthy marriage. Of course, sexuality for the sake of sex alone is another issue. Most of these traditions have problems with sex only for pleasure since it seems to be stripped (pun intended) of its deeper meaning. Extramarital and premarital sex, masturbation, and homosexuality are generally regarded as evil or sinful by most of these traditions. Thus, sex in a specific way is okay, but sex for the sake of pure sexual gratification is problematic.

Buddhist and Hindu teachings typically maintain that sex for marriage and procreation is essential. And as I have already alluded to, a number of sects find a way of embracing sexuality and sexual energy to actively engage their spiritual side. While monks in most Buddhist and Hindu sects refrain from sexual activity, for those practicing Tantric Buddhism and Yoga, sexuality is part of the path toward spiritual experiences. Utilizing the physiological aspects of sex—activating the autonomic nervous system and various emotional and cognitive centers of the brain—sexual practices can parallel the mechanisms supporting spiritual experiences.

Within an intimate relationship of marriage, sexuality and its associated experiences lead to great compassion and a blissful understanding of another person. In many ways, the ideal marriage is one in which both individuals truly understand and empathize with each other, and this is most fully expressed during the sexual act. While many of these ideas seem trite in today's topsy-turvy world, especially when almost half of all marriages end in divorce, there is clearly something to be said for the positive elements of a healthy, sexually active marriage.

---

169   West C. *Theology Of The Body For Beginners*. Ascension Press; 2004.

FINDING COMPASSION

In my prior books with Mark Waldman, we talked a great deal about trying to foster compassion within the human brain so that people can have more intimate relationships. By intimate, we do not inherently mean romance, marriage, or even a sexual relationship. We mean that human beings can form deeper connections with everyone around them—friends, colleagues, and even people we interact with on a day-to-day basis at the restaurants, stores, and banks we frequent.

So how does compassion and empathy develop in the brain and what does it have to do with sexuality? By now, hopefully the answer is somewhat obvious. As part of sexual selection in the evolutionary process, empathy stems from an ability to understand what a potential mate is feeling. The rhythmic resonance that we discussed earlier is all about trying to understand each other. It is important to understand how active and how passive we should be in any relationship. And even when it comes to sex itself, it is important to know how forceful or how gentle to be. During sex, there is typically an important rhythm between both. Being too gentle the entire time may not be stimulating enough, and being too aggressive might become painful and shut down the feelings of arousal. The perfect balance for any given pair requires a great deal of mutual empathy and understanding.

This empathic trait is not just about the physicality of sex itself, but all of the cognitive and emotional elements as well. What gets said before sex occurs requires romance, poetry, and humor in the right balance. Too much romance might seem artificial and too little romance might seem too mechanical.

All of these elements continue to balance in the brain in order to drive sexual arousal to the point of actually mating. Thus, we can see the essential nature of empathy and compassion as part of the mating process. Rituals and myths can help contribute to that sense of empathy, but it is ultimately the brain itself that helps each of us figure out how to interact with others.

Interestingly, the practice of OM specifically emphasizes the importance of this type of empathic relationship. Practitioners clearly recognize the importance of being able to assess how the other person in the pair is doing during the OM practice. The male who is stimulating the female's clitoris needs to be aware of how hard or soft to apply pressure. He needs to know whether strokes should be short or long. And with each modification he makes, he needs to be able to assess the female's positive or negative response. This is part of the reason why activity in the social, as well as sensory areas of the brain, became active during the OM practice. It turns out that it is important for the brain of each person engaged in the OM practice to be able to resonate with each other as effectively as possible.

We studied this in our brain scans and found correlations between the brain changes of the participants. We found a number of significant correlations in the change of brain activity when directly comparing the individuals in each OM pair to each other. In other words, activity changes in certain brain regions in the male subjects correlated with activity changes in certain brain regions in their female partner. In particular, there were correlations between the social and empathy areas of the brain (including the insula and precuneus). Remember that the insula sits between the emotional limbic areas and the higher cortical areas. The insula works to allow us to feel our emotions and understand them. But not only does the insula help us understand our own emotions, it helps us to feel another person's emotions as well. Thus, as the two people become attuned to one another's feelings during OM, their brains register that connection.

We further discovered that activity in the insula and temporal lobes correlated with the perceived intensity of the experience in the other member of the pair involved in the OM practice. This was true both with how female participants influenced male participants, and vice versa. That means that the brain of one person was able to interact with the other person in a way that fostered more intense experiences.

If all of this occurs during the OM practice, it stands to reason that there would be similar kinds of changes occurring in people who are engaged in the more natural sexual process. And this reciprocal connection is precisely the result of rituals, particularly mating rituals. These rituals lead to mutual connections in the brains of people engaged in the mating process, particularly when that process is successful.

These findings equate to biological proof of how sexual selection in humans can occur.

We are able to make powerful connections with potential mates through our mind, our empathy, and our compassion. And we do this in a way that fosters sexual feelings as well. In this way, sexual selection of the right kind of compassionate mind leads to mating and the passing on of these kinds of mental processes through the future generations produced.

DEVELOPING EMPATHY AND COMPASSION

We can see that empathy and compassion arise inherently as part of the sexual selection process. Both males and females need to be able to perceive and interpret what other people are feeling as they synchronize their neural circuits during the mating process.

As with many of the traits that we have discussed, empathy and compassion have neurological correlates and can also be enhanced or reduced, depending on a person's circumstances and practices and how much they are able to pay attention to and connect with another person. In my previous work, I discussed the importance of facial expressions and body language when it comes to communicating what we are thinking and feeling. It makes sense that there are important areas of the brain that are specifically attuned to observing the face and body of others. We can distinguish different types of smiles from those that are truly happy to those that are devious. We can see whether someone is feeling a bit down or is truly depressed just by looking at their face and body language.

Once the sensory information enters into our brain, our emotional centers help us to feel what the other person is feeling based on how they are expressing their emotions. But we need our emotional centers and our memory centers to help us make that link. We appear to have a set of "mirror" neurons that help us to feel and mimic what others feel. While the research on mirror neurons in the human brain is ongoing, there is evidence indicating that if I watch you smile, there is a part of my brain that smiles with you. In that way, I can know how you are feeling.

All of this makes sense from a sexual selection perspective. We need to be able to perceive exactly what another person is feeling, particularly in response to our own actions and language. We can see if somebody is responding well to us or ignoring us.

Beyond sexuality, the same processes can be applied to people in general. We can understand if a child is sad because they dropped their ice cream on the sidewalk. We can feel the anger of someone we let down. And we can feel the pain, both physical and mental, that other people feel when they are suffering from an illness or trauma. It is interesting to note that research has documented that mental pain is perceived in the same areas of the brain as physical pain—a broken heart is quite literally a broken heart.[170]

Practically speaking, the ability to empathize with others is a trait that can also be developed and learned. If we pay closer attention to other people's facial expressions, listen to the emotions in their words, and watch their body movements, we can get better at understanding what people around us feel.

The brain has the remarkable ability to continue to grow and adapt over time, learning from all of the information that it receives on a moment-to-moment basis. If we consciously focus our attention on how other people feel, the neural connections that support that ability will continue to strengthen. It is a skill that we each have to varying degrees, but it is also a skill that can be learned.

Studies of positive emotional practices such as loving-kindness meditation have shown that those practices trigger activity in the social and empathic areas of the brain, and the more a person does that practice, the more positively and compassionately they feel about others.[171] It is not clear how far each person may go in developing their own sense of empathy and compassion. However, the more a person does engage in positive emotions and beliefs, the more those beliefs shape the brain and the way they feel and behave going forward.

---

170   Sturgeon JA, Zautra AJ. Social pain and physical pain: shared paths to resilience. *Pain Manag*. 2016;6(1):63-74. doi:10.2217/pmt.15.56.

171   Gu X, Luo W, Zhao X, et al. The effects of loving-kindness and compassion meditation on life satisfaction: a systematic review and meta-analysis. *Appl Psychol Health Well Being*. 2022;14(3):1081-1101. doi:10.1111/aphw.12367.

Improving the sense of compassion and empathy can reduce stress and anxiety for the individual, and also for people around them. There are physiological effects such as altered neurotransmitters in the brain as well as reduced activity in the arousal part of the autonomic nervous system. Reducing stress and anxiety leads to improved immune function, hormone function, and brain function.

For these reasons, religious and spiritual beliefs, specifically when they espouse positive emotions, along with feelings of compassion and empathy, are likely to lead to better brain function and better mental and physical health.[172] A number of attempts have been made to incorporate positive spiritual or religious content into more traditional psychotherapeutic interventions with a fair amount of success. This makes sense given the physiological changes that occur as the result of focusing on compassion and modifying brain areas that are also involved in anxiety and depression.

Just as the pursuit of sexuality can lead to lifelong bliss between and for two partners, so too can spirituality lead to a life full of positive emotions, compassion, and empathy. Isn't this the ultimate goal of virtually every religion anyway? The trick in both circumstances is to find the right myths and rituals that can lead a person in the right, adaptive direction. And if these positive approaches lead to healthier individuals who are more likely to create long-standing relationships with many children, these positive traits should actually evolve as part of humanity. Unfortunately, the same can be true of negative approaches if they find a way to squeeze out and destroy people that hold positive emotional and compassionate perspectives. As with all things in evolution, there isn't an inherent right or wrong; it is about that which survives.

172   Koenig HG, ed. *Handbook of Religion and Mental Health.* Academic Press; 1998; Koenig HG. Religion, spirituality, and health: a review and update. *Adv Mind Body Med.* 2015;29(3):19-26; Lucchetti G, Koenig HG, Lucchetti ALG. Spirituality, religiousness, and mental health: a review of the current scientific evidence. *World J Clin Cases.* 2021;9(26):7620-7631.

CHAPTER 14

MALE AND FEMALE SPIRITUALITY

The difference in the ways of working, by which men are the actors, and women are the persons acted upon, is owing to the nature of male and female, otherwise the actor would be sometimes the person acted upon, and vice versa. And from this difference in the ways of working follows the difference in the consciousness of pleasure, for a man thinks, "this woman is united with me," and a woman thinks, "I am united with this man."

—Burton and Arbuthnat, *Kama Sutra*

THE GENDER DIFFERENCE IN SEXUALITY

Throughout this book, we have considered the relationship between sexuality and spirituality. But one of the proverbial elephants in the room has to do with how spirituality is affected not only by sex, but by sex. In this case, the second "sex" refers to gender—whether people are male or female, as well as orientation—whether people are heterosexual or homosexual. And in today's world, we can further consider how the growing variety of approaches to gender are associated with spirituality. In fact, studying differences between cisgender and transgender individuals, as well as between heterosexual and homosexual individuals, can reveal important ways in which spirituality intersects with our biology and our sexuality.

Thus, when it comes to evolution, sexuality, and spirituality, we have been touching on another point which is certainly worth mentioning in this context. As we have seen, spiritual practices and experiences appear to utilize similar brain processes as those for sexual practices and experiences because of their mutual interrelationship.

But this also sets up an interesting question about the differences between males and females. From an evolutionary perspective, there is a clear distinction primarily because females have the egg (or eggs) that requires its own form of protection. Further, especially in mammals and human beings, the female bears the children, and hence, is certain that they belong to her. Males in most animal species, and particularly in mammals and human beings, are able to impregnate multiple females, and since the males do not bear the young, they are often not as involved in ensuring the survival of those young.

The females, while being selected for by their potential male mates, are still generally the gatekeepers of the sexual process. Therefore, it is not surprising that in the large majority of species, the males are the ones with large colorful feathers and large ornaments such as antlers. These aspects of a species, based on sexual selection, help to fend off potential competitors as well as help to impress the ladies who say when and who they mate with. Females are often less colorful than the males, but certainly are very attractive to those males.

What is more important for our present discussion is that the behaviors of males and females are in many ways markedly different. Obviously, both males and females are involved in the mating and selection process, but come at it from completely different angles as mentioned in the quote at the beginning of this chapter. The males compete with each other and are far more aggressive in trying to get a female to mate with either of them. Females are typically more receptive in the process, but are far from passive. They are particularly important when it comes to making the final selection and determining the characteristics that ultimately define the species.

As mentioned in the chapter on rituals, there is frequently a great rhythmic process that exists between the males and females. As with dancing, there is typically one person who takes the lead while the other person follows. When one person is moving forward, the other has to be moving backwards. In the context of rituals, this implies that there would necessarily be differences in what both the male and female bring to the overall process.

Much like the sexual act itself, the female is typically more in the role of the receptive individual whereas the male is typically in the role of the active pursuer. In much the same way, the male sperm must pursue the female egg. Thus, at the most basic physiological level there are certain parameters that are established, based on how sexual mating actually occurs. There is a pursuer and a pursuee.

There has been evidence that this occurs in a similar manner when it comes to spiritual experiences. Women tend to describe these experiences in more passive ways whereas men are more likely to describe them in active ways. Take a look at these two brief examples. The first is from the well-known saint and mystic, Sister Teresa Avila:

> Christ has no body now but mine. He prays in me, works in me, looks through my eyes, speaks through my words, works through my hands, walks with my feet, and loves with me here.

Here she describes Christ as being the pursuer as everything happens *to her* or *in her*. While males also experience the core element of surrender, they tend to view themselves more as actors in the process. This is evident in this 55-year-old male's description of a numinous experience, documented as a component of our previously mentioned survey:

> [It] is very hard to [describe my experience]. My intention before my journey was to kneel before God. Afterwards I discovered that it was impossible because I am in God. 'God is the dancer and creation is his dance.' I am part of his dance. I can't kneel before him if I am part of him.[173]

There are also other differences in the mating and sexual process that one would expect to affect the experiences of both males and females in different ways. While it is difficult to determine precisely what male and

---

173 Institute for Mystical Experience Research and Education. I am in God. Institute for Mystical Experience Research and Education. 2022. Accessed March 18, 2023. https://imere.org/experience_story/i-am-in-god-2022/.

female animals may feel or experience during the mating process, we do have a fairly clear understanding of the differences between male and female human beings. Both male and female human beings are able to experience the pleasures of sex but frequently do so in different ways. For example, women have many erogenous zones and can find sexual pleasure from many different parts of their body. Men tend to have a primary focus on the penis. There has also been a long discussed "orgasmic problem" in human beings because men are able to achieve orgasm rather quickly, and in a singular manner, whereas women can have multiple orgasms from a variety of manners, but they often require much more time to achieve them.[174]

The process leading up to the sexual experience is also quite different in males and females. The ways in which males and females are aroused are different. Males are turned on from more sexual visual displays. Pornography is almost exclusively the domain of males, although certainly females are also stimulated by pornographic material.

Arguably, women require more romancing that can include dates, dinners, dances, gifts, music, and poetry. While some men enjoy romancing activities, they are typically less interested or require less romance for them to become sexually aroused. Males are far more sexually aroused by the appearance of the female body. It is interesting that the female body has its own type of ornaments including rounded buttocks and pendulous breasts. These help to demonstrate fertility to a male, but even so, are not required for sexual arousal.

It is important for females, in particular, to have a sense of personal connection with a potential sexual mate that includes the ability to have conversations, interactions, humor, and a sensitivity toward their feelings. These requirements on the female side force males to adapt sufficient brain capabilities in order to establish a mate. It is because of these mutual cognitive and emotional interactions that sexual selection in human beings may have led to larger brains that are capable of music, art, poetry, and ultimately the ability to tell stories and understand the universe around us.[175] For these reasons, religion and spirituality come to the fore as part of the sexual mating process.

---

174 Margolis J. *O: The Intimate History of the Orgasm.* Grove Press; 2004.

175 Miller G. *The Mating Mind.* Anchor Books; 2001.

In the end, sexual orgasm itself has a great deal of similarity from the experiential perspective. Males and females both are capable of attaining orgasm and both feel a sense of incredible arousal and bliss surrounding the experience. Research studies have shown that there are mostly physiological similarities between males and females during orgasm with activation reported in the cerebellum, anterior cingulate gyrus, insula, and dopaminergic pathways.[176] During orgasm there also tends to be decreased activity in parts of the frontal lobe similar to what we have described during feelings of surrender.[177]

Thus, if we relate sexual orgasm to spiritual experience, we might expect at least some similarities in males and females, along with a few important differences.

THE GENDER DIFFERENCE IN SPIRITUALITY

It seems on one hand that people of all genders and orientations are spiritual and have spiritual experiences. This makes sense since we know that virtually all people are able to be sexual and have sexual experiences. However, given those basic similarities, we have also learned that sexuality can be different across people. If sexuality is different between males and females in human beings, spirituality is likely to be different as well. We have already seen this in the above quotes from both a male and female describing their spiritual experiences. But let us look deeper into how males and females generally engage religious and spiritual traditions,

---

176 Komisaruk BR, Whipple B, Crawford A, Liu WC, Kalnin A, Mosier K. Brain activation during vaginocervical self-stimulation and orgasm in women with complete spinal cord injury: fMRI evidence of mediation by the vagus nerves. *Brain Res.* 2004;1024(1-2):77-88. doi:10.1016/j.brainres.2004.07; Wise NJ, Frangos E, Komisaruk BR. Brain activity unique to orgasm in women: an fMRI analysis. *J Sex Med.* 2017;14(11):1380-1391.

177 Komisaruk BR, Whipple B. Functional MRI of the brain during orgasm in women. *Annu Rev Sex Res.* 2005;16:62-86; Salonia A, Giraldi A, Chivers ML, et al. Physiology of women's sexual function: basic knowledge and new findings. *J Sex Med.* 2010;7(8):2637-2660.

practices, and experiences. To begin, many traditions establish a prominent distinction between males and females. Often, especially in the orthodox, males and females are separated. In part, this is to ensure that sexuality does not interfere with spiritual engagement. But it also ends up yielding differences in how religion is actually experienced by both males and females.

At the risk of being overly simplistic, males tend to engage religion in a more philosophical and theological manner. Males, while considering religion, typically explore large-scale issues such as the nature of free will, the nature of human consciousness, or the origins of the universe. Women tend to have a more social perspective on religion and seek to establish close personal relationships with other members of their group. Of course, males and females are interested in both sides of religion and spirituality, but there does tend to be an emphasis that is different between males and females.

In our Survey of Spiritual Experiences, content analysis revealed similar distinctions.[178] The most intense experiences for males tended to be described in broader philosophical and theological terms regarding consciousness, free will, and the creation and nature of the universe. Women tended to describe their experiences with words that focused on the family, friendship, and personal connections. In this way, religion and spirituality for women tends to be a more social process than for males.

Descriptions from our survey, as well as famous mystics, further develop this:

> Generally, my experiences have involved ecstasy beyond descriptions but which led to certainty about the divine which I would not try to even express . . . certainly questions such as: 'Do you believe in God?' are too simplistic. I would no longer say 'I believe'—because 'belief' is certainly too weak a word, I no more 'believe' in God than I 'believe' I just ate dinner.—a 35-year-old male in our survey

---

178   Newberg AB, Waldman MR. *How Enlightenment Changes Your Brain: The New Science of Transformation*. Penguin Random House; 2016.

I saw Adishesha (seven-headed serpent) opening its hood above our house, my husband, family, and myself. Adishesha said that he was there to protect us, as we are very precious. I felt that the Formless God has taken the shape of my body. I felt my Soul become one with God. I heard a voice say, "Do not light your heart using the light of others; your heart is self-luminous, and it will light up independently whenever it is necessary."—a 60-year-old Hindu woman

In the previous examples, the male is focusing on God and belief. The female is focusing on God and her family. Thus, we can see certain similarities and differences between males and females who experienced something spiritual. Both experienced something divine, but it was expressed in different ways.

In our study of Orgasmic Meditation, we found physiological differences between men and women as well. On one hand, this is expected, since the women are the receivers of the sexual stimulation whereas the males are the givers of that stimulation—much the same way as we might see in the mating process. The males needed to pay more attention to the manner in which their physical activity had an effect on the female. He needed to evaluate whether he was stroking the clitoris too hard, too soft, or in a way that was or was not achieving its ultimate goal. Although he has to be very purposeful and active during the practice, he also has to have a strong receptivity to be able to assess the female who is responding in ways he can follow. For the male, there is an intense sense of focus on the female that leads to a state of flow. It feels as if the process itself takes over and the ritualized element of the practice becomes the experience itself.

The female, who is experiencing the sexual impulse, has to be able to incorporate that feeling as part of a meditative focus. She needs to be in tune with the male as she becomes part of the experience itself and has a feeling of oneness or connectedness in the experience. In this way, she loses her sense of self as part of the process.

In our study, males tended to have decreased metabolic activity in the frontal lobes confirming the experience of a sense of surrender or flow. Women tended to have an experience of oneness or connectedness that was associated with a decrease of metabolic activity in the parietal lobes. However, there was certainly an overlap among these findings as well.

The sense of oneness and connectedness is still universal in all people, as are the ineffable, noetic, transient, and passive qualities. These are the core characteristics of almost all spiritual experiences. However, as mentioned above, women tend to express spirituality and mysticism in a more receptive manner. It comes to them. Men tend to be more aggressive in their pursuit and discuss their experiences more along the lines of how they actively engage their spirituality. Of course, our research suggests that even men will usually refer to experiences with the notion of surrender. And this is sometimes considered to be a more "feminine" side of mysticism. It is the person returning to the oneness and blissfulness of the womb.

Another distinction that has been reported is that women tend to describe their spiritual experiences in plain, everyday language, while men are more likely than the women to rationalize, systematize, number, and interpret their experiences. We have found this to a certain extent in our survey data in which women tended to discuss spirituality and mysticism in more relational ways, whereas males did so in more philosophical ways. But it must be kept in mind that these are sweeping generalizations based on the analysis of thousands of reports. We have also found that each person has a uniqueness to their experiences. Consider the following from a 30-year-old male in our survey:

> I have had one full blown mystical experience in which I lost my body and felt like everything was in me (not my ego) and I was everything. I saw through the boundaries of social rules and things people normally do. I felt a massive love towards all living things. I sensed the presence of living in plants, I could understand them (their biological growth etc., not communication or something like that). I felt like I knew everything, just that I didn't understand what it all meant. I saw that no matter what, I'll always have the people I love and appreciate, and they have me. Everything felt a lot more real than everyday life. It was like waking up from a dream. It was very clear.

In his response, he talks about social rules, people, and love in ways that are highly relational. Thus, while we might describe males as having general differences compared to females on a population basis, there are plenty of male descriptions that involve family and relationships and plenty of female descriptions that are highly philosophical and analytical. This is due in part to everyone existing sexually and spiritually along a continuum. While they might be analogous, they are not identical.

Perhaps an even bigger problem, which does not yet have an answer, is whether different experiences are truly different, or just interpreted as being different. If different people feel a "power," "spirit," "feeling of love," or "feeling of awe," are these fundamentally the same and just interpreted in different ways, or are they truly distinct? The answer is quite challenging to find because spirituality and sexuality have complex brain processes that affect emotions, cognitions, and experiences a little bit differently in everyone.

VARYING PERSPECTIVES ON GENDER AND SEXUALITY

Given everything we have discussed to this point, we might ponder whether there are any differences between spirituality and spiritual experiences in homosexual, heterosexual, and transgender individuals. If we are right in terms of understanding the powerful relationship between sexuality and spirituality, there really should not be any significant differences in their core elements. It is possible there might be population-based differences in how they are approached or interpreted, so it could prove beneficial to explore whether gay men and women generally consider spirituality in more philosophical or more relational ways. However, we would expect all people to be able to have spiritual experiences, and they should all share the same basic elements, even if there also might be some differences.

On one hand, there is not a lot of data on the spiritual experiences of gay or transgender individuals. Hopefully, future studies will help to clarify whether they experience something unique when it comes to spirituality. But, again, my guess is that there would not be any clear differences. From what we do know of the several studies that exist, homosexual individuals espouse high levels of spiritual well-being both in terms of how they relate to God (religious well-being) and how they feel about life in general (existential well-being).[179]

The results from a Barna Survey in 2009 reveal further population-based differences regarding spirituality among gay versus straight adults.[180] For example, straight adults (72%) were more likely than gay adults (60%) to describe their faith as "very important" in their life. Further, 85% of straight adults described themselves as Christians compared to 70% of gay adults. Heterosexual adults were twice as likely as homosexual adults to state that the Bible is totally accurate in all of the principles it teaches; two-thirds of heterosexual adults believe the single, most important purpose in life is to love God with all your heart, mind, strength, and soul, significantly higher than the 50% of homosexual adults who embrace the idea. Finally, about half of straight adults and one-third of gay adults contend that their life has been greatly transformed by their faith.

In terms of beliefs about God, one of the largest differences noted in the survey was that 71% of heterosexual adults have an orthodox, biblical perception of God, but just 43% of homosexual adults do. In fact, an equal percentage of gay and straight adults hold a pantheistic view about a higher power feeling that God can refer to many different perspectives, including personally achieving a state of higher consciousness.

The data are interesting since, on one hand, there seems to be substantial differences between gay and straight individuals, but in looking at the numbers, there seems to be lots of people from both sexual orientations that embrace religion and spirituality. Certainly, the negative beliefs of many religions and treatment of homosexual individuals by such religions is likely the cause for lower rates of religiosity among gay individuals. But it is important to note that homosexual individuals generally have a very robust spiritual life. And related studies indicate that spiritual pursuits in

---

179   Tan PP. The importance of spirituality among gay and lesbian individuals. *J Homosex.* 2005;49(2):135-144.

180   Barna. Spiritual Profile of Homosexual Adults Provides Surprising Insights. Barna. 2009. Accessed March 18, 2023. https://www.barna.com/research/spiritual-profile -of-homosexual-adults-provides-surprising-insights/.

homosexual individuals derive from the "motivation to make sense of one's place in the world especially in light of societal misunderstandings and intolerance to LGBTQ+ individuals."[181] Everyone is looking for their sense of meaning and purpose—the brain's self-maintenance system trying to understand their place in the world.

The limited data available suggest that transgender individuals also have highly spiritual lives. Lisa Salazar, in her research published in the book *Transparently*, says she has discovered that transgender individuals "are more than twice as likely to be spiritually touched by the beauty of creation, seven times more likely to be thankful for blessings, and two-and-a-half times more likely to feel selfless caring for others."[182]

All of this implies that the basic elements of spirituality hold regardless of a person's sexual orientation. This further shows the importance of the link between sexuality and spirituality. It doesn't really matter what turns you on, it just matters that you are turned on. Whether you are gay or straight, you have a brain that experiences sexual arousal and sexual orgasm. So, it makes sense that everyone should have the ability to embrace spiritual experiences even if they do not fully embrace religious dogmas. And while there may be differences in what makes up spirituality for each person, the data continue to point to great similarities in terms of the feeling of oneness, the feeling of surrender, and the transformative elements of clarity and intensity that comprise these amazing and universal experiences. Consider the following survey response from a 37-year-old female:

> The Spirit took me to my home. It took me to places where my family was, and it allowed me to see them from above as though hovering and looking down. We went to various places where various family members were just doing whatever they were doing at

---

181   Halkitis PN, Mattis JS, Sahadath JK, et al. The meanings and manifestations of religion and spirituality among lesbian, gay, bisexual, and transgender adults. *J Adult Dev* 2009;16: 250-262.

182   Salazar L. *Transparently: Behind the Scenes of a Good Life*. Independently Published; 2011.

the actual time. I observed them and had powerful feelings of guilt and bliss mixed as I realized it was all just part of The Great Whole. Never ending and never beginning. I realized how small yet how important my part in life was.

IS RELIGION AFRAID OF
SEX? AND SHOULD IT BE?

God has given us many faiths but only one world in which to coexist. May your work help all of us to cherish our commonalities and feel enlarged by our differences.

— Jonathan Sacks, English rabbi and philosopher

Faith grows when it is lived and shaped by Love.

— Pope Francis

RELIGION AND SEX REVISITED

We are now ready to readdress the original question about why religion appears to not like sex, at least for the act of sex itself. It is because sex shares the same biology with religion. We have seen how the biology of spirituality is connected to the biology of sexuality. And we have seen this from a neuroimaging perspective, specifically as it pertains to the study of spiritual practices such as Orgasmic Meditation and others. We have also seen how evolutionary forces yielded the biological connection between sexuality and spirituality by mutually supporting natural selection through the processes of self-maintenance and self-transcendence. Sexual selection has also been essential in connecting sexuality and spirituality by enabling women and men to connect through a mind capable of producing and responding to language, music, beliefs, and rituals.

While religion tries to go one step further in terms of powerful experiences, and often does, religion and sex are still intimately tied to each other. This new research connecting spirituality and sexuality has wide ranging implications for how we understand ourselves as human beings. Historically, theologians have debated the distinction between our biological and spiritual sides. In Saint Thomas Aquinas's famous work, *Summa Theologica*, he considers the *actus hominis* and the *actus humanus*. The *actus hominis* refers primarily to our biology and our natural drives for eating, sleeping, and sex. The *actus humanus* refers to the actions of human beings that require thought and intention. He argues that we are in a constant struggle between the two, although both are essential for our being. His perspective on sexual pleasure is intriguing since on one hand, it is a natural part of the body, but when engaged only for pleasure or toward excess, it can become sinful. Aquinas acknowledges that sexual activity should not occur when engaged with spiritual pursuits such as specific holidays or contemplation and prayer. Sexuality distracts human beings from appropriate spiritual pursuits. More specifically, "In man's fallen state resulting from original sin, sexual pleasure is not submissive to reason, but powerfully absorbing the mind, irresistibly distracts it from spiritual realities."

Just how concerned should religion be about sexuality? Here is an intriguing story from our Survey of a woman raised in the Mormon faith that brings forth this tension between the sexual and spiritual, and this is certainly not limited only to Mormonism, but as we have seen, to virtually all traditions in one way or another:

> I was raised in a strict Mormon environment. Mormonism controlled every aspect of my life—who I married, what I wore, who I voted for, who I associated with, etc. I even served a Mormon mission for a year and a half learning Spanish and serving in the ghettos of Los Angeles. I was told that angels were protecting me and so I freely walked in the most dangerous of areas—convinced that I was being watched over by God ... [I]n my forties I was excommunicated from my church. Most of my family, friends, cohorts, etc., abandoned me. I eventually came not to believe in the concepts of my religion (including not having sexual relations outside of marriage). I had sexual relations with someone who I was engaged to be married to. I then became very sick with an illness. Of course, family and

friends claimed I was being punished for my "sins." They told me I must confess to my bishop. I did and was sent to a court. There I was asked all kinds of questions with a man in the room taking copious notes. My bishop was there, as were his counselors. The questions included about where and how often I had had sex . . . It was devastating at the time. My husband (we have been married for two years) went through something similar. He was a bishop in the Mormon Church when he came home to find blood all over his house. His son had tried to commit suicide because the Mormon Church told him he was "a son of perdition" because he is gay. He lost community, reputation, family, friends. . . . I cannot believe how my entire life was controlled by someone else's thought system. When I was excommunicated, I went through a time of absolute wonderment in actually trying to think for myself. I studied many books and authors including "A Course in Miracles," Byron Katie, Eckhart Tolle, David Hawkins. . . . I studied Eastern philosophies. At one point I went to a funeral for a prominent Mormon neighbor named Clara. I sat in the audience and sobbed and shook. On the stand were my bishop and some apostles (apostles are very famous in the Mormon Church and are believed to be just like the 12 apostles of Jesus— with the same power of "the priesthood"— which women, by the way, are unable to hold). The fiancée with whom I was sexually involved was, of all things, an apostle's son. He had been excommunicated himself several years before. I had been so severely rejected by my community and I had been told in no uncertain terms by the bishop on the stand at the funeral what I was—"a total and complete sinner"—that I cried uncontrollably. My mother looked over at me on the bench and said, "I know why you are crying. It is not over the death of Clara, it is over the way you feel so hurt and lost and rejected and judged." I nodded yes. I abruptly started to shiver. . . .

The Mormons' condemnation of sex outside the sanctified boundaries of the church mirrors other strands of Christianity (although Mormonism and Christianity differ in some important respects). Galatians 5:19-21 (ESV) encapsulates the perils flesh poses to the spirit: "Now the works of the flesh are evident: sexual immorality, impurity, sensuality, idolatry, sorcery, enmity, strife, jealousy, fits of anger, rivalries, dissensions, divisions, envy, drunkenness, orgies, and things like these. I warn you, as I warned you before, that those who do such things will not inherit the kingdom of God." We see here the irreconcilable difference in certain aspects of the Christian doctrine between the spiritual aspirations and carnal temptations. This is similarly seen in the other monotheistic traditions of Judaism and Islam. These religions, particularly in the more orthodox denominations, have strong feelings about sexuality, forbidding extramarital and premarital sexual activity. Even Buddhism and Hinduism generally are against sexual activity outside of marriage. And when you include concepts such as the caste system that dates back thousands of years in the Hindu tradition and guides who you can marry, you can see how sexuality is highly regulated.

As we have also learned, there are other religious and spiritual perspectives that embrace sexuality and even use it to foster spiritual experiences. There are ancient Cults of Venus, Tantric sects (with modern examples such as Osho), and various esoteric strands of Daoism and Kundalini yogic practices. All of these have found ways of embracing and using the energy and arousal that people feel during sexual stimulation to bring about spiritual experiences. Given what we know about the arousal and quiescent systems of the body, it makes sense that generating a hyperarousal or hyperquiescent state, even if done sexually, can lead to powerful feelings of ecstasy or bliss.

The previously shared story of the Mormon woman eventually had a happy, and incredibly spiritual, ending. She had a vision of Clara and through that vision, she had an incredible experience:

> Suddenly something other-worldly occurred. I saw Clara at the end of the hallway. She came towards me into my room. I recognized her because of her outer form. I say outer form because she was translucent, yet color filled, if that makes any sense. Clara somehow filled me with what she feels wherever she is now. Suddenly I felt as if someone had placed a needle about two to three inches long in each and every pore over my entire body, starting at the top of my head

and ending with the bottom of my toes. The needles had something in them that was the essence of pure unadulterated ecstasy. It was a joy that I have never felt in this earthly existence, and I am certain that it does not exist at the earthly level of vibrational being. The needles tingled full of warm bubbly unconditional love. I was in a state of complete euphoria and exultation that I have never before or since experienced. I was involuntarily smiling from ear to ear. I lay in the midst of this pleasure and rapture as the needles continued to tingle and pour warm, pure, syrupy, liquid affection into my veins. The veins carried it swiftly to my major organs and I breathed tender compassion. My blood became a river of sweet adulation. I then realized that if there were a drug that could reproduce that feeling—I'd be on it twenty-four-seven. I know beyond a shadow of a doubt that this feeling was ethereal—from another realm.

The last part of this experience brings us to a final point about what these experiences truly represent. There is a realness about them that convinces people to embrace a different view of reality. Specifically, there seems to be an experience that is so different from the everyday material reality we all experience. This is what those core elements lead to. The experience is too intense, too clear, too unified, and too transformative to be anything but supernatural. Or is it?

THE PROBLEM OF REALITY

The idea that sexuality and spirituality use the same brain circuits is of fundamental importance for understanding how we as human beings work, and how we interact with the world around us. But as we have also considered throughout this book, this relationship leads to some fundamental questions: "Does the sexual brain create the spiritual or does the spiritual create the sexual brain?" Knowing what we now know, the divisiveness between the sexual and spiritual may be at odds with logic because they share similar biological processes. In fact, we might ponder whether the ultimate answer is that they have created each other, arising from mutually evolving processes in the brain. In this way, sexuality and spirituality develop together, and consequently, work together to provide us some of our deepest ideas about our own being and about reality itself.

However, there is arguably a far more profound issue which is the epistemological question: Where is reality itself when it comes to spiritual experiences? We addressed this a bit at the very beginning of this book, but now we can delve into this problem a bit more.

In all of my research, the primary driving question is: "How do we know what is real?" This is asked from a scientific, philosophical, theological, and spiritual perspective. And by "real," what we are primarily talking about is the reality around us and within us. Each of us has a perception and belief system about reality. You might be a religious person. You might be a scientist. You might be both or neither. But the bottom line is that all of our brains are in the same boat.

We are looking out on an infinitely large universe with access to an infinitesimally small percentage of what is in that universe, and asking our brain to figure out with some reasonable degree of certainty what is going on.

Scientifically, we might conclude that reality is made up of only the physical stuff we see. The atoms and molecules, the energy and forces, all make up everything that there is. In this materialistic world, there is very little room for anything outside of the physical or material. Some scientists acknowledge that even physical reality might be more complex than that. When we get into things like quantum mechanics and cosmology, we discover that there are a great many mysteries that seem to go beyond the traditionally perceived physical world. Of course, most scientists would argue that anything that we cannot measure at the moment is still not supernatural, only the natural that has not been fully explored or studied.

Philosophically, we might turn to reason or phenomenology to tell us what the universe is made of. Perhaps reality is nothing more than all of the phenomena that exist or perhaps there are ways in which we can explore the logic or experiential aspects of reality that tell us something about the nature of that reality. The great philosophers such as Aristotle, Plato, Kant, Hume, Spinoza, and Husserl have all been trying to unlock the mystery of reality from various angles. I have argued in previous works that most philosophical systems derive from specific brain processes often taken to extremes.[183] Thus, Aristotle talked about the four types of causality that pervade the universe and make it work. But perhaps that was just his brain's causal processes functioning in overdrive to find causality at the root of all things. Or perhaps philosopher Edmund Husserl, the father of phenomenology, had overactive sensory processes that made him realize that the world is based on all of the ways it can be sensed or experienced. Of course, the philosophers were not basing their approaches on the brain itself, but they were certainly using their brain in the course of contemplating their philosophical systems.

And what of theology and religion? The religious and spiritual view of reality starts with the supernatural—with God or some universal consciousness from which all of reality is derived. It should not be a surprise that we believe in things we can't see. After all, we can't see most of what is in the universe. This perspective goes a step further to assume that anything in material reality must have come from the creative force of the supernatural, usually God. Science and philosophy are part of God's creation, not the other way around. In this view, reality is created and sustained by God. Or, from the Buddhist or Hindu perspective, reality is created and sustained by a universal consciousness or Brahman. Although science challenges this view at times, most deeply religious individuals will state that since we can never know reality for certain, we must accept faith as the path toward comprehending that reality.

These different approaches are often at odds with each other, but sometimes can be mutually supportive. It is interesting that some interpretations of quantum mechanics rely on the conscious measurement of a particle or wave in order to have it coalesce to be observed. Does this mean that consciousness and material reality are actually connected? There is still much debate about such a possibility. Some religious individuals fully embrace science noting that there should not be anything inconsistent between the two. The Dalai Lama said, "If scientific analysis were conclusively to demonstrate certain claims in Buddhism to be false, then we must accept

---

183 Newberg AB. *The Metaphysical Mind: Probing the Biology of Philosophical Thought*. CreateSpace Independent Publishing Platform; 2013.

the findings of science and abandon those claims."[184] But such statements do not imply so much that Buddhism might be wrong; they imply that science and spirituality must find some way to move together in our exploration of reality.

A NEW WAY OF FINDING REALITY

I hope that the field of neurotheology that was used throughout this book helps to bridge the gap between the *actus hominis* and the *actus humanus*, and between sexuality and spirituality. In the brain, we have the core structures that are involved in basic biological functions, particularly sex. The structures include the brainstem, hypothalamus, thalamus, and limbic system. These structures are involved in our basic drives and maintain our survival and the survival of human beings as a species. These brain structures also regulate the autonomic nervous system which is essential for mating and sexual experience.[185] And they are primarily responsible for our emotional processes.

The structures associated with the humanistic aspects of us are the higher cortex, or neocortex (because it is more newly evolved in *homo sapiens*). Even from an evolutionary perspective our neocortex is far different than that in any other animal in terms of size and complexity of the various parts of the brain such as the frontal, temporal, and parietal lobes. It is no wonder that this neocortex has enabled us to engage in philosophy, morality, and science, as well as the arts and creativity. Perhaps most important for our discussion here is that the neocortex enables us to consider and connect with our concept of God or ultimate reality.

In the brain, the cortex and the core structures are constantly in counterbalance with each other. When we are thinking a great deal, we tend to suppress our emotions. And vice versa, when we become emotional, we tend to suppress our thinking. However, there are times when our

---

184   Dalai Lama XIV. *The Universe in a Single Atom: The Convergence of Science and Spirituality*. Morgan Road Books; 2006.

185   Amen D. *The Brain in Love*. Three Rivers Press, 2007.

thoughts and feelings combine in powerful ways such as during intense spiritual or mystical experiences. We should also note that there are several brain structures that form a kind of fulcrum between the core structures and the neocortex. As we have seen, the anterior cingulate gyrus and the insula represent these two main structures that physically lie between the core structures and the neocortex, thus connecting our emotions and our thoughts. These are the structures that can help us put words and thoughts to our emotions as well as emotions to our words and thoughts. Ultimately, all of these brain structures, and the networks connecting them, appear to come together to help us have consciousness. But similar to our questions above: "Does consciousness come from the brain or does the brain come from consciousness?"

Our neurotheological research of spiritual practices that alter our consciousness, such as religious rituals, prayer, or meditation, shows a potential way to answer these fundamental questions and find the right balance. The right balance depends on blending all parts of ourselves in a manner that generates emotions like compassion and love, and combines them with thoughts and ideas about all of humanity and the interconnected nature of the universe. In this way, we do not find either our consciousness or biological side to be a problem, but rather to be fundamental parts of who we are and how we connect to the universe. By embracing the emotional, cognitive, sexual, and spiritual, this neurotheological research will hopefully point a way to the next phase of human evolution and enlightenment.

How long will this take and how far will we need to go? God only knows!

ACKNOWLEDGEMENTS

Both spirituality and sexuality ultimately lead to a sense of community and there have definitely been a number of people who have played a part in helping to develop the ideas in this book, too many to list in detail. My late colleague, Dr. Eugene d'Aquili was a pioneer in this area of research and laid the foundation for exploring how rituals and myths link the sexual and spiritual parts of ourselves. Our many fascinating conversations still resonate with me today. This work could not have happened without him. My other colleagues have helped me to be able to perform the cutting edge research that seeks to understand spiritual practices and experiences including my neuroimaging mentor, Dr. Abass Alavi, and my current colleague in the study of integrative medicine, Dr. Daniel Monti. My friends and family have always contributed to my work, knowingly or not, simply by humoring my conversations about the brain, consciousness, philosophy, and theology. And most importantly, by always encouraging me to explore the nature of humanity and nature of reality.

INDEX

symbols
    fertility, 2
    phallic, 2–3, 4
    religious, 34–35
Symposium, The (Plato), 6

tantric sects, 4–5, 8, 176, 197
temporal lobes, 40, 78, 134, 189, 201
Ten Commandments, 167–68
Teresa, of Avila, Saint, 184
territorial imperative, 166
testosterone, 28, 136, 159, 162, 167, 174
thalamus, 52, 55, 201
theology, 195, 200
    See also neurotheology
Thomas Aquinas, Saint, 195
tobacco, 86
toxins, 137
transcendent function, 127
traumas, 96–97, 98, 109, 111, 125, 136, 137–39, 145
    See also abuse; post-traumatic stress disorder (PTSD)
trust, 109, 110, 145, 146, 161, 168, 174
2001: A Space Odyssey (movie), 152

unconscious, 126–27

unity. *See* connectedness; oneness; wholeness
universe
    creation/origin of, 3, 4, 6, 17, 40, 59, 62–63, 85, 155, 200
    understanding of, 40–43, 83, 85, 198–202
    See also reality

Varieties of Religious Experience, The (James), 122
vasopressin, 90
Venus (cult), 48–49, 197
violence, 9, 148–63
    religious, 148–52
    sexuality and, 156–63
virgin birth, 4
visions (religious), 105

warfare and wars, 149, 152
    sexual violence and, 157–58
wholeness, 126, 127, 202
witch hunts, 140, 148
worship, 48–49, 58, 59, 60, 168, 170
    phallic, 3

Yoga Nidra, 100

ABOUT THE AUTHOR

Andrew Newberg is Director of Research at the Department of Integrative Medicine and Nutritional Sciences at Thomas Jefferson University Hospital and Medical College. Dr. Newberg has been particularly involved in the study of mystical and religious experiences throughout his career, in addition to the use of neuroimaging studies in the evaluation of neurological and psychiatric disorders. He is considered a pioneer in the field of neurotheology which seeks to link neuroscience with religious and spiritual experience.

Dr. Newberg has published over 250 articles, essays, and book chapters. He is the author or coauthor of 14 books, translated into 17 languages, including the bestselling *How God Changes Your Brain* (Ballantine, 2009) and *Why God Won't Go Away* (Ballantine, 2001). He has presented his work at scientific and religious meetings throughout the world and has appeared on *Good Morning America*, *Nightline*, *ABC World News Tonight*, *Book TV*, National Public Radio, London Talk Radio, the Discovery Channel, the History Channel, the National Geographic, the BBC, *Fresh Air*, and the nationally distributed movies, *What the Bleep Do We Know?* and Bill Maher's movie *Religulous*. His work has been written about in *Time*, *Newsweek*, *Discover Magazine*, *Reader's Digest*, *The Los Angeles Times*, *The Washington Post*, and *The New York Times*.